The Politics of Crisis Reporting

Learning to be a Foreign Correspondent

The Politics of Crisis Reporting

Learning to be a Foreign Correspondent

John Crothers Pollock

PRAEGER SPECIAL STUDIES • PRAEGER SCIENTIFIC

Library of Congress Cataloging in Publication Data

Pollock, John Crothers
    The politics of crisis reporting.

    Includes index.
    1. Foreign news. 2. Reporters and reporting.
3. Foreign correspondents. I. Title.
PN4784.F6P6   070.4′33   81-15350
ISBN 0-03-044336-9   AACR2

Published in 1981 by Praeger Publishers
CBS Educational and Professional Publishing
A Division of CBS, Inc.
521 Fifth Avenue, New York, New York 10175 U.S.A.

© 1981 by Praeger Publishers

123456789   145   987654321

Printed in the United States of America

To the memories of

my maternal grandmother
Flora Wilkin Reib (1880–1962)
and
my brother
Craig Reib Pollock (1947–1972)

Contents

Introduction

How do journalists decide what to write about during a crisis? How do the personal experiences and life histories of foreign affairs reporters affect their work? The purpose of this book is to explore the way learning patterns and attitudes formed prior to critical events influence reporter perspectives on crisis reporting. Specifically, how do the experiences of a lifetime affect the way foreign correspondents view their roles as reporters, their relations with government officials, and their perspectives on East-West conflict?

From a survey designed to explore those questions, this study maps new intellectual terrain in at least two ways: First, it follows journalists over the entire course of their lifetimes, asking how experiences and choices occurring both early and later in the lifecycle affect professional perspectives on reporting. Second, it explores the impact of both occupational and non-occupational, formal and informal experiences on a reporter's acquisition of professional reporting perspectives.

Several studies focus on the effect of different types of news organization characteristics and constraints on reporter attitudes. But in the author's judgment, *The Politics of Crisis Reporting* is the first systematic effort to measure the impact of influences both inside and outside news organizations: not only organizational factors — such as income, supervisory responsibility, and amount of teamwork; but also family and educational experiences undergone prior to selecting a career, and adult friendship and source choices. By uncovering the enduring importance of choices made early in a reporter's career, this study suggests that the journalism profession generally and crisis reporting in particular are profoundly affected by heroic individuals making critical decisions. Reporters are not products of news organizations alone. Intimate decisions exert a decisive impact on the professional attitudes of journalists.

The Politics of Crisis Reporting is not a book about "politics" as a set of pressures and bargains surrounding journalists as they attempt to sort out the complexity of dramatic events. This study adopts a much broader perspective, viewing politics as a process for what David Easton called "the authoritative allocation of values." If politics refers to difficult choices among competing values, then it is useful to ask how influential groups, in this case foreign affairs reporters, acquire the values they hold. This survey focuses on deeply rooted orientations and learning experiences that precede the immediacies of crisis reporting.

Some accounts, such as Evelyn Waugh's *Scoop,* are masterful in dramatizing the serendipitous excitement of a correspondent's life and craft. Others, frequently authored by scholars, examine systematically the "output": the articles and editorials printed by wire services, newspapers, and magazines. Where the novelist looks for individual excitement and exception, the scholar typically searches for universal reporting patterns. Between those two approaches lies a chasm of ignorance.

Despite careful research, scholars know relatively little about the making of a professional foreign affairs reporter. Sometimes, thorough group profiles are drawn, as in the work of Wilhelm (1963), Kleisch (1975), and Peterson (1978) in the United States and Tunstall (1972) in Great Britain. At other times operating "codes," "conventions" or "routines" are documented, as in the work of Galtung and Ruge (1965) and Rosengren (1977) in Sweden; Elliot and Golding (1975) in Great Britain; Robinson and Sharpes in Canada (1977), and Batscha (1975), Cohen (1963), Knudson (1974c), and Lent (1974) in the United States. Still others compare regular patterns in foreign affairs reporting in one country with that in another, cataloguing the amount of "attention" media in one country give to affairs in another (Gerbner and Marvanyi, 1977). Researchers are typically curious to know how much coverage major media in an industrial country give to countries in the Third World. Such studies are excellent at pioneering universal or shared behavior patterns common to most foreign correspondents. But they reveal little about how much variation exists in the attitudes and behavior of those correspondents.

The differences journalists display may be as significant as their similarities, especially under conditions of crisis reporting, characterized by surprise, the need for quick decisions, and a high level of threat. In such circumstances, what much of the United States, many parts of the world, and responsible policy makers learn about a crisis in its initial stages may depend on a few reporters covering that region for major news organizations such as *The New York Times* or the Associated Press. In the initial phases of a "critical event," when happenings are ambiguous, opinions unformed, and policy amorphous, the personal attitudes of a handful of correspondents may exert influence of global proportions on the shaping of public and official responses. This study considers three attitude clusters of critical importance in crisis reporting.

1. *Attitudes toward reporting as an occupation.* To simplify a complex choice for illustrative purposes, how much do journalists maximize speed, breadth, and accuracy in their reporting roles, and how much do they admire investigative, interpretive reporting?
2. *Attitudes toward government officials.* How much do reporters regard officials as colleagues, and how much as adversaries?
3. *Attitudes toward international conflict.* How much do reporters consider international intervention and conflict as natural, and how much do they consider them unusual circumstances? How much are local and regional issues viewed in the broader context of East-West conflict?

The attitudes foreign affairs journalists hold regarding appropriate occupational roles, relations with officials, and orientations toward international conflict may make a significant impact on the way news receivers form perspectives on new crises.

A special caution is necessary. In measuring the attitudes of foreign affairs reporters, this study suggests that journalists may display several deeply held orientations affecting their outlook on crisis reporting. To search for enduring attitudes and orientations displayed by reporters is not, however, to claim that attitudes introduce a systematic "bias" into what reporters write or what their employers print about a given crisis. What a reporter writes is a product of many complex conditions and events, including the nature of the crisis, the reporter's knowledge of the region's history, the availability and variety of sources, level of polarization of different viewpoints, global location of the crisis, strategic interests of the United States, and news value to U.S. readers. What a reporter writes may also depend on the level of confidence and trust he enjoys among editors and publishers.

Further, regardless of a reporter's cables, what his employer decides to print is typically the product of far more than the accumulation of a reporter's orientations toward appropriate reporting and international roles. Decisions about editing, quantity of material to use (and in the case of newspapers and magazines, how much correspondent news as against wire service copy to use), and news value contained in a particular kind of story are the result of an intricate set of processes and assumptions so complex that their systematic description continues to puzzle scholars. In the context of myriad influences affecting those in a news organization who decide what to publish, the personal orientations of reporters may often amount to no more than a pinch of seasoning in a very large stew.

Yet compared to other professionals posted abroad, such as executives and government officials, foreign affairs reporters have astonishingly direct access to the public and to policy makers. And in the first stages of a crisis, where a journalist on the spot may have more immediate information than almost any other source, a foreign correspondent, traditionally among the most trusted reporters, may enjoy a striking amount of direct contact with a wide range of publics and authorities.

The influence of several reporters during the war in Vietnam comes immediately to mind, for example, in the reporting of: David Halberstam of *The New York Times;* Neal Sheehan of the UPI; Malcolm Browne of AP, and of course, Seymour Hersch, who illuminated the massacre at My Lai. In such circumstances, the personal orientations of individual journalists may assume enlarged proportions, serving as a frame of refernce for the interpretation of conflicting accounts.

If the personal orientations and beliefs of correspondents are important, then a significant question arises. How are those attitudes acquired? This study adopts a special approach to that question: a "socialization" or learning approach. That approach makes two assumptions. 1) Early learning in childhood or early adulthood has a major impact on attitudes and beliefs that are significant in adult and late adult experience. 2) Informal learning experiences with family or friends have an impact on professionally relevant attitudes that is potentially as large as or larger than that exerted by formal occupational experience. Indirect learning may be as potent as direct occupational learning in the acquisition of professionally useful attitudes. This socialization or early adult learning approach resembles what psychologists often consider an "Eriksonian" approach. Named after the distinguished psychologist Erik Erikson, it draws attention to critical moments and their resolution early in an individual's life, typically in adolescence. It suggests that decisions made early in the life cycle have a substantial influence on later decisions of great magnitude.

Pioneering this approach, Erikson has illuminated, among others, the lives of Luther (*Young Man Luther,* 1958) and Ghandi (*Ghandi's Truth,* 1969). The analysis developed in this book suggests that the learning experiences of the Luthers and Ghandis of the world may be undergone as well by those whose grasp on immortality is somewhat less secure but nevertheless critical in their contribution to the formation of foreign policy: foreign affairs reporters.

Based on interviews with over 100 journalists with experience reporting on Latin America for U.S. print media, *The Politics of Crisis Reporting* challenges several accepted views about the way foreign correspondents work. The following findings contradict conventional wisdom:

1. Younger reporters are not substantially more likely than older reporters to act as "watchdogs" on the behavior of officials;
2. The least experienced area specialist reporters — those with few years reporting on a region and with few friends in a region — are actually more likely than those with regional experience to examine thoroughly the assumptions of policy makers either in host countries or in the United States;
3. The types of sources journalists contact do not, in themselves, exert a clear influence on reporters' views regarding professional reporting.
4. The experiences journalists undergo early in their lives regarding schooling and career path choices are far more important than later adult experiences in explaining why some journalists become more professional than others.

Every scholar owes debts of gratitude, and I have been guided by many willing helpers. For financial support in the early phases of the study, I wish to thank the Joint Committee on Latin American Studies of the Social Science Research Council and American Council of Learned Societies for two grants (summer, 1975, and the academic year 1977–1978) and for the scholarly advice offered by the Latin American staff director, Louis Wolf Goodman. Additional financial support was offered several times by the Rutgers Research Council, through both summer grants and partial support for a sabbatical arrangement.

Funding apart, I have been blessed with the interest and support of several scholars and friends. Torry Dickinson, Joseph Somma, and John Leggett encouraged my early research in mass media and social change. Christopher Guidette combined a reporter's skepticism and a friend's gentility to provide needed critical perspectives. Irving Louis Horowitz held aloft the canons of social science, reminding me that a social scientist's first commitment is to answer theory with systematically gathered evidence. Vera Green and Helen Safa, both anthropologists who served as directors of the Latin American Institute at Rutgers, were exemplary scholars devoted to expressing Latin America's concerns for American readers. Hewson Ryan and Richard Fagen encouraged me to present preliminary thoughts to significant audiences. Foreign policy scholar and creative genius Lawrence Falkowski shared many of the professional dilemmas involved in completing this study, and to Timothy Perper I owe an incalculable debt of gratitude. Not only did he contribute countless hours as a friend and biologist to discussions of the study, but he also volunteered scores of evenings and weekend afternoons to computer analyses of the survey results.

For invaluable guidance in preparing the survey questionnaire, I want to thank Michael Aronoff, James David Barber, Bernard Cohen, John Crewdson, W. Phillips Davison, James Nelson Goodsell, Al Hester, Jerry Knudson, Gary MacEoin, Jack MacLeod, John McNelly, Dan Nimmo, and Leo Rosten. For agreeing to write letters introducing my questionnaire to reporters and editors interested in Latin America, I am grateful to Tad Szulc, distinguished former corespondent for *The New York Times,* and James Thomson, Jr., Curator of the Nieman Foundation at Harvard University. I learned a great deal from Jerry Knudson and Terri Shaw, fellow members of the first Committee on the U.S. Press and Latin America of the Latin American Studies Association. Herbert Gans made useful comments on a draft of the manuscript. For professional encouragement to continue scholarly work in mass communication research, I am especially indebted to Dan Hahn and Helen Cairns of Queens College, City University of New York; Richard Hixon, Livingston College, Rutgers; and Jerome Aumente of the Journalism Resources Institute at Rutgers. For their extraordinary patience and support I owe an extra bouquet of appreciation to Peter Dahlgren and Marilyn Frasier. And for their loyal encouragement at all points in my own lifecycle, I am grateful to my parents — John Crothers Pollock, Jr., and Jane Reib Pollock — and my sisters, Mary Pollock Shilling and Amy Pollock.

Several people participated in converting questionnaires responses into a finished manuscript. Annabel Litman and Kathleen Kane helped prepare the questionnaire codebook and with Pam Friedberg converted raw answers into coded data. Several drafts of the manuscript were typed with professional dispatch by Dawn H.R. Frederick with Mary Kathryn Harrity, Laura McClory, Phyllis Moditz, Diane Swartz, and Bruce Holley.

This list of acknowledgements would be incomplete without a special tribute to the professionals who made this study possible: the foreign affairs reporters and editors with experience in Latin American reporting who responded to a lengthy questionnaire. To the more than forty busy individuals who consented to probing personal interviews at the Associated Press, United Press International, *The New York Times, The Wall Street Journal,* the *Washington Post,* the *Washington Star,* and the *Los Angeles Times,* a special salute. Their willing cooperation helped me understand how much dedication, integrity, and hard work are required to perform as professional news gatherers reporting on foreign affairs.

The Politics of Crisis Reporting

Learning to be a Foreign Correspondent

PART ONE

1

A Dilemma in Foreign Affairs Journalism

A foreign correspondent in a third world country reports social unrest so faithfully that he is expelled. A correspondent in a war zone reports discouraging news for U.S.-backed forces and incurs the wrath of the President of the United States. The reporter's employer decides to retain him in that post in order to avoid charges of government interference. Another correspondent for a weekly in the same war zone resigns when his editors convert the unfavorable material he writes into an optimistic story.

Each of these events presents correspondents and news institutions with professional and ethical dilemmas of major significance. Writing stories about urban squatters in Chile immediately prior to the election of President Salvador Allende in 1970, *New York Times* Pulitzer-winner Malcolm Browne risked the anger of Chilean authorities and was declared *persona non grata*.[1]

Keeping correspondent David Halberstam in Vietnam despite presidential anger, *The New York Times* risked disruption of patterns of cooperation between journalists and officials (Aronson, 1970:202). Deciding to change entirely the thrust of Charles Mohr's reporting from Vietnam, *Time* magazine was faced with the resignation of one of its distinguished correspondents (Mohr was later employed by *The New York Times*). (Aronson, 1970:200–202).

These examples of personal and institutional conflict are not presented in order to exalt the performance of New York's most distinguished newspaper. Rather they suggest that crisis conditions pose problems of major significance and compel journalists at every level, from correspondent through publisher, to make choices of transcendent importance both for journalism and for the formation of foreign policy.

How do foreign affairs journalists approach professional and ethical choices? What assumptions do they carry? What special dilemmas and responsibilities do they confront? Have correspondents changed their professional roles and beliefs as foreign policy has changed? These questions are central in learning how foreign-affairs journalists behave under stress.

A Special Occupation with Special Responsibilities

Corespondents confront difficult choices. Freedom of speech is sanctified by the First Amendment, but the responsibilities which accompany that freedom are given little attention in the formal canons of journalism. James C. Thomson, Jr., curator of Harvard's Nieman Foundation, recently reviewed prevailing ethical codes for journalists. He concluded that all are inadequate as guides to socially "responsible" journalism. (Thomson, Jr., 1978). Existing codes have done little to implement what a Special Commission on Freedom of the Press, the "Hutchins Commission," suggested in 1947. It recommended that the press project a "representative picture of constituent groups" in society and "clarify the goals and values of society." (Commission on the Freedom of the Press, 1947, quoted in Thomson, 1978:8.)

That recommendation poses a special dilemma for journalists reporting on foreign affairs. One of their major functions is the transmission of information on foreign societies and governments. They are supposed to convey a representative picture of different groups and predominant values in those societies. At the same time, foreign correspondents are expected to perform similar tasks for their own society, illuminating their own country's values and goals by reporting on the activities of others in a framework comprehensible to home-country readers.

How much should the aspirations of their country of assignment govern what journalists write? And how much should they adopt the vision provided by their own news institution or country? How can journalists be faithful to the events they experience and yet remain loyal to the legitimate concerns of the public and employer they represent? These questions concern all who work abroad, be they diplomats, businessmen, or reporters. The U.S. State Department, recognizing the possibility that Foreign Service officers may identify with the interests of the country of assignment, routinely shifts personnel among different regions of the world. Editors similarly shift reporters from one "beat" to another to diminish excessive identification with source interests. (Roshco, 1975:114.)

Whatever its importance for other occupational groups, for journalists working abroad, the question of divided attention and loyalty presents a special problem. A businessman or other private citizen who becomes over-zealous in protecting his home company's interests may affect company policy and indirectly the perception of his corporation and country in the host country. But the influence of a few such individuals, unless well coor-dinated, is unlikely to have a vast impact on public policy at home and abroad. A foreign-service officer may similarly become committed to a par-ticular policy of supporting or critiquing home-country policy, but the bureaucratic layers through which his recommendations must pass provide numerous checks on individual judgment and wisdom.

A foreign correspondent occupies an altogether different occupational and social space. Because relatively few news institutions in the United States field foreign correspondents — and their number is declining (Kliesch, 1975) — because the work of a single correspondent in a single location may be shared with hundreds of papers due to news chains and wire-service subscriptions, each journalist reporting from abroad affects the views of vast numbers of citizens.

Compared to most other occupations, the occupational hierarchy of journalism is shallow. Foreign correspondents in particular have more autonomy than other reporters in selecting stories and sources. (Tunstall, 1972, in McQuail, 1972.) There are few layers of judgment between a foreign affairs reporter and the public. Some editors may examine a reporter's prod-uct before it reaches article form in a newspaper. But foreign affairs cor-respondents are typically among the most trusted reporters, having served long apprenticeships before assignment overseas. (Wilhelm, 1963:147–168; Yu and Luter, 1964: 5–12; Hohenberg, 1964; Bogart, 1968:293–306; Kleisch, 1975.) Further, other reporters cannot be sent to cover the same story on short notice because distance and cost discourage it. The typical result is that news institutions accept the bulk of reports filed from the field.

Those reports are conveyed directly to the reading public, for whom newspapers (along with television) are probably the major source of infor-mation on foreign affairs. Yet journalists, protected by the First Amend-ment, are not directly answerable to any governmental or citizen group for what they write. Foreign correspondents wield vast informational influence, but they seldom can be held accountable for it. As sociologist Michael Schudson points out in *Discovering the News: A Social History of American Newspapers,* "nothing in the training of journalists gives them license to shape others' views of the world." (Schudson, 1978:9).

Under ordinary circumstances, individual influence may not appear to be visibly important. Journalists can be expected to report from the field at least partially what editors and readers expect to read about any particular region. For example, several studies suggest there is substantial continuity or "consonance" between industrial countries' cultural perceptions of the third world and reporting about that region. (See Galtung and Ruge, 1965:64–91; Elliott and Golding, 1973, in Boardman and Groom, eds., 1973; Lent, 1977: 46–51). Under conditions of crisis, however, when policy makers must make rapid decisions, or when public perceptions and support or disaffection regarding policies are crucial, journalists may exert a gigantic influence on events.

Under such circumstances, journalists and news institutions function not simply as profit-making enterprises or as information gatekeepers, but rather as public institutions with public power and concomitant public responsibility. The First Amendment was framed to recognize the special, public role of news media in a representative political system. Given its central role in that kind of system, how can journalists reconcile reporting about "constituent groups" and social "goals and values" abroad with the interests and perceptions of editors, publishers, and readers at home? How can socially "responsible" reporting on foreign affairs be encouraged?

If the wisdom of the Founding Fathers is to be followed, we can assume that no single group or agency, or even the government itself, can be entrusted with the responsibility of supervising the activities and articles of journalists. Some other occupational groups have avoided government supervision through efforts at self-regulation. Among the most obvious of these are the professions of law, medicine, and university teaching, all of which have complex mechanisms for encouraging socially responsible behavior. Indeed, the very concept of "profession" suggests a sense of autonomy from outside regulation, a commitment to act in a socially responsible manner, and a willingness to determine the boundaries of that behavior.

The capacity of foreign affairs journalists to engage in socially responsible journalism may therefore depend on the way they address their occupation as a serious "profession." How useful is the concept of "profession" in describing the issues foreign correspondents face? Specifically, how "professional" are journalists, and what constraints do professional values place on political (foreign policy) involvement? How can the professional orientations of foreign-affairs journalists help explain reporting on crises abroad?

Professional Dilemmas

To assert that foreign-affairs reporters — correspondents, editors, and editorial writers — are involved in a profoundly political profession is not to claim anything new or surprising. Most journalists would probably agree that they and their associates contact politicians and officials frequently, exchange information, and depend on one another for myriad favors, trading background information for the publicity of a trial balloon, bargaining political secrets for favorable coverage of some issue or personality. Yet this admission of politial involvement is often coupled with another, that reporters are in some sense "objective," that they report the news according to well established and hallowed canons of professional practice.

How comfortable are politics and professionalism as bedfellows? A prominent statement by a president of the foreign correspondents' primary association, The Overseas Press Club, illustrates how controversial the term "professional" can be for working foreign affairs journalists. In his introduction to the 1975 *Membership Directory* of the Club, issued every five or six years, Jack Raymond wrote:

> Are we better off with *talented newsmen* who acquire working knowledge of specialized information or with *knowledgeable specialists* who acquire working knowledge of journalism's techniques? . . . I suspect that if we 'professionalized' journalists with specialized education, we would actually eliminate any claim that journalism might have to being a profession. The learned professionals would use journalism as a technique, but journalists themselves would shrink in number (emphases added).
>
> Yet the press in America was never expected by the Founding Fathers to be one of the 'learned professions' such as medicine, theology, and the law, inevitably constricted by standards, regulations, and even license from higher authority. The press was encouraged by the Fathers of the Constitution to challenge authority, to be undisciplined and even to be somewhat irresponsible.
>
> Thus, *the professionalism of newsmen is based* to a large degree *on its antiprofessionalism* (emphasis added), on standards of excellence and honesty rather than formally established codes and patterns of practice which too often are reduced to bureaucratic 'respect for higher authority.'
>
> And that is, of course, why the Overseas Press Club . . . nevertheless continues year after year to serve not a profession so much as a basic, social ideal — "freedom of the press," freedom, even, to be unprofessional. (1976 Overseas Press Club Membership *Directory,* p. 6).

The association of "professionalism" with bureaucracy, control by outside arbitrary authority, and diminished freedom might be assumed prevalent among foreign affairs reporters (correspondents, editors, and editorial writers). But the virtuous individualism championed by Jack Raymond, in the absence of a code of professional guidelines, can itself permit "outside" interference with the practice of foreign affairs journalism. Freedom from formal constraints does not necessarily signify freedom from informal, outside influences, especially when that influence is targeted at selected individuals or news institutions. The fragmented nature of professional journalism permits contracts of convenience between a variety of government and business groups, on the one hand, and reporters and news organizations on the other, ranging from the exchange of casual background information to the specific contracts of the Central Intelligence Agency. For concerned journalists, these compartmentalized arrangements raise serious questions about professional autonomy and integrity.

Reports in *The New York Times* (December 28, 1977–January 3, 1978) about the investigations of the House Subcommittee on Intelligence Oversight reveal that these liaisons of convenience are disturbing to at least some prominent journalists. The House investigations explore not only the direct or indirect employment of journalists by government agencies such as the Central Intelligence Agency (See Trento and Roman, 1977:44–50). The investigators are also concerned with C.I.A.-produced or -inspired "disinformation" printed abroad, then entering the United States either directly or indirectly, absorbed or retransmitted by correspondents for U.S. news organizations.

The C.I.A. issued new regulations on November 30, 1977, stating, in effect, that it would not recruit journalists accredited at any "U.S. news service, newspaper, periodical, radio, or television network or station, for the purpose of conducting any intelligence activities." (C.I.A., December 2, 1977). But testimony presented by authoritative sources in the U.S. journalism community before the Subcommittee on Oversight (of the Permanent Select Committee on Intelligence) on January 5, 1978, revealed widespread concern about the Agency's continued recruitment and employment of journalists working for non-U.S. news media. Eugene Patterson, President, the American Society of Newspaper Editors (ASNE), and Clayton Kirkpatrick, Chairman of that Society's International Communication Committee (and Editor of the *Chicago Tribune*) condemned in the strongest possible terms the C.I.A.'s refusal to discontinue employing journalists working abroad. ("Statements" by E. Patterson and C. Kirkpatrick, 1978.)

Although the word "professional" may be disparaged when it connotes government interference, U.S. journalists exhibit considerable "professionalism" in their warnings about government intervention in the process of printing news on foreign affairs. Journalists might have sounded the alarm earlier, before their relations with government agencies became public knowledge, but their concern compels serious attention.

Defining a Profession

Some of these conflicting claims and the dilemmas they present might be clarified by understanding more about what a profession is. The historical growth of professional associations can be examined as a guide. Compared with the development of other occupational groups, journalism exhibits several similarities with other "professions." Using Wilensky's list of historical stages through which an occupational group moves in becoming established as a profession, journalism certainly qualifies. In these stages, the occupational group: (1) begins to pursue an area of work as a full-time profession; (2) establishes a training school; (3) forms a professional association; (4) agitates politically to win legal support for the right of members to control their work; and (5) in its capacity as a professional association promulgates a formal code of ethics (Wilensky, 1964:137–158).

In a recent systematic national sample of more than 1,300 practicing journalists, Johnstone, Slawski, and Bowman concluded that journalism met these criteria, each one in differing degrees. Regarding training, for example, it is often expected that recruits to a given field must be exposed to a body of abstract knowledge that is the particular province of the profession. There is little consensus in journalism about what abstract propositions should be taught or whether any are necessary (only about three journalists in five have finished college). (Johnstone, et al., 1976:99–100.) In addition, largely out of concern for First Amendment protections, considerable professional fragmentation prevails: "There is no single qualifying association in journalism, and the functional diversity which characterizes the news media in general is thus paralleled in professional associations." (Johnstone, et al., 1976:101).

Yet there are clusters of evidence that suggest that "professionalism" means something, that journalists "identify" as professionals and exhibit a number of traditionally professional values. A third of all respondents in the Johnstone, et al., sample concentrate the majority of their informal social relationships within the professional community. Most journalists are found to place high value on: professional autonomy and freedom from supervision, the hallmarks of a professional; commitment to public service; and a sense of "calling" to a career, what Kornhauser termed the "belief that the development and exercise of expertise is worthy of a lifetime and carries its own reward." (Johnstone, 1976:108–111.)

Journalism does not appear to exhibit an extremely elaborate code of ethics which prescribes boundaries of acceptable behavior nor, as in the example of disbarment from the legal profession, formal sanctions applied to those who violate professional norms. But reporters do make reference to some standards of appropriate conduct. Although journalism is not an occupation that boasts the lengthy training periods and elaborate certification thresholds of law, medicine, theology, or college teaching, it is nevertheless a profession with a system of codes, ethics, and serious expectations.

At the center of journalism's professional core lies a notion of integrity that implies a relatively high degree of autonomy from the machinations of politics. Thus, in the United States, most news media can be expected to take pride in, or at least render lipservice to, such ideals as: a low degree of government interference with media operations; a low level of partisan commitment (e.g., few explicit organized connections to political associations such as parties); a small amount of integration between media elites and political elites (e.g., few personnel overlaps and exchanges); and a legitimizing creed that values a "distancing" of media from the pressures of "external interests and a fidelity to the internally generated norms of the profession itself. "Creeds promoting this kind of insulation may be composed of such elements as: belief in the primacy of service to audiences or readers (over and above duties owed to organized political authority), belief in the watchdog function of journalism, and the need to adopt an adversary stance." (See Blumler and Gurevitch, 1975:165–193.)

If journalism is to cloak itself in the mantle of professional respectability, if it is to wear the crown of professional integrity, then a legitimate question arises: how much involvement in politics contaminates the cherished capacity of journalists to present news in a professional manner? How much political involvemnt is too much? When is a journalist not a journalist at all, but rather a representative of some special interest, private or governmental? Does journalism display occupational boundaries, or is it a rather permeable, porous category, capable of penetrating and being penetrated by other occupational specialties? These questions of professional ethics and definition are disturbing for journalists and non-journalists alike, but they are especially worrisome in reporting on foreign affairs.

Reporters and Officials: Overlapping Domains

Foreign affairs reporters enjoy a high degree of organizational autonomy, are difficult to challenge, interact with people in myriad occupations and positions of power, and exercise vast influence. Each of these attributes permits foreign affairs reporters large arenas of choice about professional and personal involvement with officials and politicians. Each attribute also invests reporters with special capacities for authority and influence.

Foreign affairs reporters, in particular foreign correspondents, enjoy a special kind of autonomy. British social scientist Jeremy Tunstall cautions that as employees of news organizations mostly concerned with domestic news, the degree of correspondent control over "story-use" (processing, altering, or not using stories after the specialist has gathered them) is relatively low, and level of story-choice (the selection of stories to be covered) is only about the same as other specialist newsgatherers (e.g., in sports or fashion). Yet, foreign correspondents tend to come from elite backgrounds and to exhibit precocious, meteoric careers, enjoy high status within the journalism profession, and in their daily work as newsgatherers benefit from a considerable freedom derived from distance and responsibility for covering a wide range of issues (Tunstall, 1972; 1974). U.S. and British journalists demonstrate similar social and occupational characteristics.

(Bogart, 1968:293–306). Indeed foreign correspondents are sometimes charged with covering an entire country or region: the correspondent in Lagos, Nigeria, with all of central sub-Saharan Africa; the reporter in Buenos Aires with the entire "Southern Cone" of Latin America. In such an occupation, intersection with political careers or even mutual, if temporary, immersion might not be unexpected.

Editors, editorial writers, and publishers concerned with foreign affairs are also in positions of political interest, access, and visibility. Sometimes political contacts occur at the highest levels; sometimes communications occur at a level one step below President to publisher. In *The Kingdom and the Power,* former *New York Times* reporter Gay Talese wrote that:

> Lyndon Johnson kept in touch with *Times* executives in various ways. Sometimes he communicated through intermediaries; at other times Johnson himself picked up the telephone and called a *Times* editor. . . . (On one occasion Johnson personally telephoned John B. Oakes, then the *Times* editorial page editor, and) informed him he was making Thomas Mann, the Latin America expert, assistant secretary of state. Oakes agreed that Mann was a good choice, and an editorial favorable to Mann later appeared in the *Times.* (Talese, 1966:124.)

Whatever the level of contact, the integration or cooperation among foreign affairs media elites and political elites is high and significant, as James Reston explains in a book published in the late sixties, *The Artillery of the Press: Its Influence on Ameican Foreign Policy:* "(People who write news) are usually dealing with news as the post office delivers the mail, and when officials and reporters perform this cooperative service, which is what they do most of the time, they are undoubtedly an influential combination." (Reston, 1966:64).

Reston further notes reporters also assist governments and influence foreign policy in more oblique ways. "For example, officials seldom like to talk about this — reporters are constantly used to transmit to foreign governments, through press, radio, and television, those officials' views which the administration in Washington does not want to put in formal diplomatic communications." (Reston, 1966:64.) Should anyone question the importance of these remarks, it should be remembered that "on some big matters the State Department informs (Reston) almost automatically, as it would the representative of a major power. (Kraft, 1958:123.)

This friendly cooperation between the press and officials might be assumed to reveal a high degree of mutual dependence and influence. James Reston disagrees. He acknowledges "the press has great influence on American foreign policy." (Reston, 1966:63.) But he also contends it is an influence that only has effect when "things are going badly." (Reston, 1966:63.) Reston documents a natural alliance between reporters and foreign diplomats in Washington, but he hastens to add that it is "preposterous" to suggest reporters have a "decisive" influence in the field of foreign policy. (Reston, 1966:63.)

The gentleman may be too modest. Major news media are crucial in setting foreign affairs agendas for public discussion because: (a) they affect foreign government perceptions of our foreign policy; (b) they set standards for foreign coverage by other media outlets throughout the United States; and (c) they constitute an almost unchallengeable source of information on foreign affairs for most U.S. citizens. *The New York Times* occupies a special place of influence among U.S. news organizations. One State Department press officer suggested that "if the *Times* ran a piece about American policy toward Costa Rica and it was all cockeyed and came from a postal clerk, it would still take at least an assistant secretary to convince the Costa Ricans it wasn't true." (Kraft, 1958:126.)

The *Times* and the wire services, together with a few other papers, also constitute a standard, an ideal against which editors throughout the country judge both the composition and importance of foreign affairs news (Cohen, 1963). The news judgments of the *Times* and the wire services are both transmitted by the wire services, as well as by the *Times*'s own news service. For deadline and promotion conscious news people elsewhere, it is far safer to follow the leaders than to disrupt the consensus created by agreed trend-setters. (See Breed, 1955:283; and Schiltz, Sigelman, and Neal, 1973: 716–721.)

The abundant exchanges among officials and journalists concerned with foreign affairs have significant consequences for domestic readers and therefore for the public context of foreign policy. News media influence is politically weighty, not simply because few other sources of foreign-affairs information are available to the public, most of which has not read many books on foreign affairs or traveled abroad. That power is indeed important, but what gives the media special clout is their unusually concentrated nature. A small number of individuals and news organizations wield vast influence, an influence which empirical studies demònstrate capable of perpetuating disturbing stereotypes about world regions.

Latin America is an instructive example. One systematic sample of evening news broadcasts on the three major U.S. television networks over a three-year period (1972–1974) discovered a striking tendency to associate Latin America with violence. A cross-regional comparison of the eighteen coded subject categories reveals one of them, "crime and terrorism," receiving an extremely high proportion of attention when broadcasters deal with the Southern Hemisphere. Over the three-year period, "crime and terrorism" constituted about 18 percent of the coverage of Western Europe and about 14 percent of reporting on Eastern Europe, with Third World regions such as the Middle East receiving about 10 percent in that category, Asia (excluding Indo-China) 5 percent, and Africa about 8 percent. Yet at least 67 percent of the coverage of Latin America, about two-thirds, falls into the category of crime-terrorism. Further, the proportion of coverage devoted to "accidents" (where less than ten people die) in Latin America amounts to 3.2 percent, exceeding the sum of that category's mention for all other regions of the world combined (Hester, 1976). Latin America may suffer a comparative advantage in the international exchange of stereotypes, depicted as a region more violent by far than any other.

It might be contended that perhaps Latin Ameria is indeed more violent than other regions and that news media merely mirror regional discrepancies. One careful study of wireservice relays, however, reveals that although only about 25 percent of the news U.S. wire services in New York receive from Latin America is related to violence or terrorism, the proportion of such news relayed to the U.S. public by the New York gatekeepers constitutes at least 50 percent of all news transmitted about Latin America. (Hester, 1971:29–43; 1974: 82–98.) Some tendency may exist to select news partially for its violent content when that news emanates from somewhere south of the United States. The same pattern docs not hold for Africa, however. If one considers how many years were required to receive information on genocide in Idi Amin's Uganda in the U.S. press, information more readily available in various foreign newspapers, an impression is confirmed that U.S. news media exhibit great variation in reporting events from different regions.

For example, a cross-national study comparing coverage of different parts of the world in the newspapers of the world's major regions concludes that the U.S. press "under-reports" news about Latin Ameria more than the Western European or Eastern European and Soviet press. (Gerbner and Marvanyi, 1977:52–66.) The importance of wire services magnifying reports on violence is underscored further when it is learned that between 70 to 90 percent of foreign news printed in the United States is received from one of our major wire services (i.e., Associated Press, United Press International, and Copley). The largest contributor of Latin American news is, by far, the Associated Press, accounting for between 50 to 70 percent of wire service material reported used by editors. (See Hester, 1974; Schlitz, et al., 1973.)

If news media are not "decisive" in foreign-policy formation, as Reston insists, they are certainly not many categories below that in setting foreign-policy agendas both abroad and at home. The weight of *The New York Times* was captured by Gay Talese, who considers it a paper where each day:

> . . . millions of words a minute, some thousands of which penetrate a large, fourteen-floor factory on Forty Third Street off Broadway (The New York Times Building), where each weekday afternoon at four o'clock — before it is fit to print, before it can influence the State Department and perplex the president and irritate David Merrick and get the ball rolling on Wall Street and heads rolling in the Congo — it is presented by *Times* editors to one man, the managing editor (then) Clifton Daniel. (Talese, 1966:2.)

Crisis Journalism: How Do Reporters Respond?

The professional dilemmas of foreign affairs journalists are not simply troublesome questions for a small group of people in a particular occupation. The high degree of cooperation between officialdom and foreign affairs journalism, coupled with the vast influence wielded by the latter, invest the process of foreign affairs news production with a sobriety and significance of vital concern to all citizens. A small number of people, many of whom, at the editorial and publishing levels, engage in frequent communication with one another, may produce a relatively standardized, apparently consensual viewpoint on events abroad and thereby make some foreign-policy options seem more appropriate or logical than others. In concluding one of his chapters on *The Press and Foreign Policy,* Bernard Cohen summarizes this problem of "power concentration" succinctly:

> The correspondents for the wire services and for the few newspapers that maintain an independent foreign affairs coverage follow a path that is narrowed at the start both because it proceeds within the framework of what they understand editors and publishers to want by way of variety and amount of foreign affairs news, and because it is subject to collegial definition of what the news is at any given moment. Beyond this initial influence on the shape of foreign affairs news as it ultimately appears in the newspaper, there is the extraordinary significance of the editorial choices, the judgments of importance made by a comparatively few people, especially in the news agencies, and in what are sometimes called the "quality" media. Their decisions constitute a powerful thrust toward the standardization of news, national as well as international, in a country that has no truly national newspaper to do the job. (Cohen, 1963:131.)

The twin observations of influence concentration and news standardization should in themselves incite investigators to learn more about those who produce and distribute news judgments. But general statements may not reveal a great deal about the *process* of foreign affairs news production. Influence concentration is not difficult to ascertain, and even a cursory reading of major newspapers in the United States reveals frequent reporting on foreign news in similar ways. If such findings are essentially valid, then it is not difficult to conclude that high levels of communication among small numbers of journalists promote consensual coverage of news abroad. It is also easy to extrapolate a corollary proposition: high levels of communication among foreign affairs reporters promote relatively homogeneous views of U.S. foreign policy.

To the extent these assumptions and products of conventional wisdom about reporting are correct, it is not difficult to find evidence for an obvious explanation: considerable good will, close friendships, and mutual respect between foreign affairs officials, especially diplomats, and reporters stationed abroad. W. Phillips Davison, who has studied these interactions for many years, observes further that some foreign correspondents and diplomats are members of a "sub-system" that he calls a "diplomatic reporting network" involving exchanges of friendship and a system of unwritten rules, observable when someone is excluded from the network for breaking one of these rules (e.g., revealing a confidential source or revealing the terms of delicate secret negotiations). (Davison, 1975:138–146.) Levels of integration between foreign affairs officials and reporters are indeed high, the resulting standardization of news on foreign affairs and foreign policy not surprising.

Historically, however, the degree of agreement between reporters and officials has not always resembled a sea of unruffled calm and punctillious manners. Disagreements have surfaced, especially in times of transition or crisis. The war in Vietnam is of course an obvious example. It was certainly one of the most widely and thoroughly reported wars in history, bringing each day's events into the television sets, and therefore living rooms, of millions of citizens. It was the "first war" for thorough television coverage. "There were 10,000 sets in the United States in 1941; at the time of Korea there were 10 million; and at the peak of the Vietnam War 100 million." (Knightley, 1975:410.) It is not clear whether television, however much it may have dramatized the war, actually ignited anti-war sentiment. Public opinion and media manager opinion samples provide mixed results, some even suggesting that electronic media coverage was related to *support* for continued U.S. involvement. (Knightley, 1975:410–415.)

Yet if Vietnam television coverage is considered both in the context of some of its major sources of stories (*The New York Times* and wire services), and in the context of the immense amount of coverage critical of the U.S. presence, then it appears reasonable to call the news media critical both in content and impact. David Halberstam of *The New York Times,* Malcolm Browne of the Associated Press, and Seymour Hersh, then a free-lancer, won Pulitzer prizes for their coverage of a "losing" war or a war fought on behalf of an unpopular South Vietnamese regime.

Certainly the South Vietnamese government and Spiro Agnew credited U.S. journalists with the erosion of U.S. support. (See Aronson, 1970: Chapts. 13–18; on Agnew, see Aronson, 1972: chapt. 1.) Coverage of the Tet offensive, beginning in January 1968, clearly affected Eugene McCarthy's decision to run in the New Hampshire primary and the decision of President Lyndon Johnson on March 31 not to seek re-election. A recent two-volume work by Peter Braestrup on coverage of the war focuses explicitly on Tet and blames the U.S. press for reporting the invasion of the U.S. embassy in Saigon and the North Vietnamese capture of Hue for almost a month as "victories." Braestrup considers that coverage a turning point in the war. (Braestrup, 1977.) And it is widely remembered that press articles on the My Lai massacre about one year later dramatized U.S. capacity for atrocities in a direct, personal way.

Peter Knightly maintains that it was "not until Vietnam (that) the war correspondent (began) to emerge as a partisan for truth and compassion." (Knightly, 1975; dust jacket.) That assertion is certainly debatable. But Vietnam probably represents one of the most prolonged periods of conflict between officials and journalists over an issue of surpassing importance in U.S. history. It is precisely the nature of that relationship, that between officials and reporters, that concerns us in this investigation.

Vietnam, a crisis of major foreign-policy dimension, revealed a variety of roles played by journalists in their relations with government officials. From the reporter who traveled with infantry units and carried a gun to the critics who were denied re-entry visas by the South Vietnamese government, a range of roles impinging on official proclamations and actions were performed by foreign correspondents. At home, some editors were more angry about atrocity stories than others, some closer to official policy than others. Whatever they learn, and however they make decisions, it is clear that individual foreign correspondents can make a substantial difference in determining what the public reads about foreign affairs, and to some extent, what the State Department and President decide concerning foreign policy in conditions of uncertainty.

The Importance of Individual Reporters

The preceding discussion can be summarized by referring to several assumptions that guide this study of foreign correspondents.

1. Foreign affairs journalists are capable of exerting vast influence

Because there are so few foreign correspondents, and because their number is diminishing rapidly as each news organization cuts costs, each individual foreign affairs journalist wields substantial influence. A few individuals covering large regions of the world write and transmit information to enormous populations in North America and elsewhere. This concentration of influence is potentially more powerful than that exercised by counterparts engaged in other careers abroad.

U.S. diplomats and businessmen must report through numerous layers and buffers before their opinions become visible to the public. The foreign affairs journalist, by contrast, traditionally among the most trusted reporters, has far more direct and immediate access to opinion-makers and the public. Checked mainly by his editor, occasionally a publisher, and commissioned to write about broad topics of paramount social, economic, and political concern, the foreign correspondent enjoys relatively unhampered access to many of those who shape opinion in the United States: those who read newspapers. Correspondents therefore perform critical roles: affecting foreign perceptions of our foreign policy; setting standards for foreign coverage throughout the United States; and constituting a major source of information on foreign affairs for many U.S. citizens.

What journalists write may carry substantial weight under conditions of crisis

Foreign affairs journalists are sometimes charged with producing stories that are so similar as to be labeled "standardized." Some correspondents themselves refer to a "herd instinct" among reporters, who may reach a consensus on topic selection and story presentation. Given their capacity for influence, tendencies among foreign affairs journalists to form or depart from a news consensus are significant for the reading public and foreign-policy makers.

Officials dissuaded journalists from releasing advance knowledge about the Bay of Pigs invasion and were later called to task for failing to convey that information to the public. (Bernstein and Gordon, 1967; Aronson, 1960: Chapt. 11.) Some reporters credit that episode with warning *The New York Times* about the pitfalls of automatic cooperation with officials and with a later important decision, made in the face of government opposition, to publish the "Pentagon Papers," revealing a great deal about official assumptions and actions during the war in Vietnam.

Journalist willingness to join or to depart from a consensus on foreign-policy perspectives was critical in forming orientations toward foreign policy in Vietnam. Whether one regards them as heroes or villains, it is not difficult to argue that the dissident reports or photographs of David Halberstam, Seymour Hersh, Charles Mohr, Neil Sheehan, and Malcolm Browne made a difference to foreign-policy makers and, ultimately, to U.S. presidents. James Reston contends that the press has inflence only when things are going badly. To the extent that widespread uncertainty in foreign affairs is the equivalent of "things going badly," the press may acquire considerable influence under conditions of uncertainty and crisis.

Vietnam is not simply an exceptional case study, it is an illustrative example of what a few journalists can accomplish if they persist in disagreeing with official policy. Since consensual reporting on foreign affairs is considered rather routine — politics stops at the water's edge — departures from that consensus are noticeable and may represent signals of concern. Under conditions of crisis, every journalist and article may be monitored closely by opinion sharers, bestowing unusual power on individual reporters and editors.

Foreign affairs journalists face difficult professional choices

Because their influence as individuals is potentially gigantic, journalists in foreign affairs confront serious choices. Expressed in general terms, journalists are often compelled to balance the need to cooperate with sources in order to acquire information with the journalist norm of autonomy from outside influence. More specifically, how can journalists gain sufficient confidence from government and business sources in order to gather accurate information and yet maintain an appropriate professional distance from such groups? How much cooperation with official and corporate sources threatens the freedom of journalists to serve as "adversaries" and "watchdogs" against abuses of power?

In foreign affairs reporting, how much cooperation with U.S. officials prevents journalists from providing the public with a clear array of foreign policy choices? How much should the aspirations of the country of assignment influence what journalists write? And how much should correspondents adopt the vision provided by their own news institution or country? How much attention should reporters abroad pay to "socially responsible" journalism, projecting a representative picture of different social groups, along with their goals and values, and how much attention should be directed toward illuminating the values and goals of home-country readers and policies? These are some of the difficult choices faced by correspondents reporting on foreign affairs.

Journalists lack clear codes of conduct to guide their decisions in periods of crisis

The reporting choices confronting correspondents are not comfortable in any circumstances, but under conditions of duress, they are even more difficult: more readers and policy officials can be influenced by individual reporters during crises than at other times. During moments of foreign-policy uncertainty, almost every article written by a major wire service or major newspaper representative may be examined with the care a fortune-teller normally lavishes on the subtleties of tea leaves. Yet for all their clout, reporters are curiously offered little formal guidance to help them resolve professional dilemmas.

Foreign correspondents may retain an awareness of general codes of journalistic ethics, but such codes are remarkably vague and, as James C. Thomson, Jr., curator of Harvard's Nieman Foundation, has observed, inadequate as guides to socially "responsible" journalism. (Thomson, 1976.) Prevailing codes warn against transgressions but seldom offer positive advice about what constitutes excellent journalism. Reporters are cautioned to stay away from the "bad" but are seldom given clues about what it means to be "good."

Some other occupations seek to instill a sense of the "good" in their practitioners through long periods of formal training. Law, medicine, theology, and university teaching all require aspirants to pass through long periods of training and apprenticeships before admission to partnership or colleague status. Journalism, by contrast, requires no such lengthy training period nor are there formal examinations or licenses to certify admission to practice. As a result, journalists as a whole are given less formal exposure to professional guidelines and norms than are those in more traditional professions.

This absence of formal standards and training poses a special problem for foreign affairs journalists in particular. They must not only consider their professional tradition of autonomy from special interests, they must also think about the foreign-policy stakes and goals of their home country, along with growing aspirations for more national autonomy or for a more equitable distribution of political, economic, and social goods among a growing number of countries. The traditional professional dilemmas of journalists are rendered even more difficult to resolve by the complexities of reporting on foreign affairs.

In the absence of elaborate professional training and clear codes of conduct, the attitudes of individual journalists toward their work, their sources, and foreign policy assume special significance.
Correspondents do not make decisions in a vacuum. They are constrained by the expectations of publishers and editors, the views of colleagues, and the routines and expectations surrounding reporting on foreign affairs. But under conditions of crisis, when previous guidelines count for less and events move quickly, reporters may be compelled to rely chiefly on their own resources.

How do correspondents learn to make choices whose impact is so telling that their very existence poses questions challenging the professional integrity and self-definition of serious journalists? Do reporters learn to make significant choices in piecemeal fashion, changing professional selections and values for each crisis? Or do they, as this study expects, form routinized norms and procedures, regularized methods for making professional choices over time, across an array of crises? Do journalists exhibit distinct patterns in learning professional values concerning foreign affairs reporting?

This study represents an effort to begin answering these questions, focusing on the attitudes of individual journalists. Each reporter's attitudes and orientations are considered important not in themselves, but as examples of the way reporters resolve ethical and professional dilemmas. Since individual correspondents and editors wield vast influence, their orientations toward their profession, toward officials, and toward East-West relations may have a significant bearing on what the public learns about disturbances throughout the world.

In this exploration of individual attitudes, a special caution is necessary. Some variation in professional perceptions is natural. No matter how well reporters are trained in the techniques of "objective" reporting, no matter how well they balance different accounts, consult authoritative sources, or display all the hallmarks of thorough, professional journalism, reporters are expected to exhibit some variation in professional orientations. This is not to presume that all individuals will be totally different, for some discernible patterns transcending individual differences are likely to emerge. To expect the appearance of differences is not to denigrate the talent and ingenuity of journalists, but rather to assume that individuals functioning in distinct social and occupational contexts are likely to behave and write differently from one another. The preceding assumptions permit the development of a special approach to the study of crisis reporting, an approach presented in the next chapter.

Notes

1. From Interview with Malcolm Browne, New York City, June 26, 1978.

2

Learning Professional Reporting Roles
A Socialization Approach

The Importance of Pre-Crisis Learning

If individual journalists are important in the transmission of foreign-affairs information, then it is essential to examine the way they learn to become reporters. To suggest that this learning process is significant is to focus on the conceptual glasses journalists bring to their tasks. In carrying a large amount of intellectual baggage to reporting on crises, journalists may resemble official decision-makers in their tendency to shape foreign perspectives or policies in predisposed directions during ambiguous situations. If established frameworks, intellectual baggage, and predispositions strongly affect reporting on crises, a discussion of two facets of learning is useful: the legacy of prior experience and the impact of social context.

Prior Experience

Prior experience is frequently studied as a significant factor affecting foreign-policy decision-makers. It may influence decisions made by foreign affairs reporters as well. Prior experience may govern the choice of historical axioms selected by individuals for application to immediate crises. (May, 1962: 653–667.) James Rosenau, for example, draws attention to "because of" motives, those which provide reasons for decisions as developed by individuals "in a vast array of prior experiences during childhood and adulthood." (Rosenau, 1971:264.) Glenn Paige argues that in a crisis the propensity to supplement information with past experience increases as the crisis intensifies. (Paige, 1968:47.) For these scholars and for Lawrence Falkowski, who has reviewed the literature on foreign-policy decision-making in detail, crises are "unplanned events during which the need for information increases dramatically." (Falkowski, 1978:21.) Fred Greenstein, the authority on political psychology, observes that under such conditions "ambiguous situations leave room for personal variability." (Greenstein, 1969:50.)

The importance of prior personal experience as a guide to crisis decision-making is summarized by Falkowski:

> In a crisis time is short and an element of surprise is present. In that situation, the decision-maker will seek as much information as possible and supplement that information with past experience. In effect, personal experience becomes an inexpensive and available source of information . . . (P)ast experience will indicate that incoming information is most relevant and how it should be interpreted." (Falkowski, 1978:22.)

To suggest that prior personal experience is important is to assert something special. Personal experience is obviously significant in any decision. To place special emphasis on it, however, is to elevate its importance over other factors assumed present in foreign affairs decisions. Some scholars argue that immediate interaction patterns of policy makers determine the outcome of foreign-policy decisions. That assumption leads some researchers to concentrate on "situational" variables, such as information flows inside different groups and on group loyalties of individual decision-makers. (Snyder, Bruce, and Sapin, in Rosenau, ed., 1969:201.) Other scholars assume that an individual's status and role in an organization predict decisions and that an "organizational approach" best accounts for foreign-policy decisions.

These factors may be significant in some foreign-affairs decisions, but under conditions of severe crisis, the personal past may acquire substantial significance. A crisis, according to Charles Hermann, is a situation that:

1. threatens high-priority goals;
2. restricts the amount of time available for response before the decision is transformed; and
3. surprises the members of the decision-making unit by its occurrence.

Threat, time, and surprise all have been cited as traits of crisis . . . (Hermann, ed., 1972:9.) Crises are likely to present reporters with sharp constraints on decision-making time and on information searches. In such instances, reliance on prior personal history is of overwhelming importance and merits special attention.

Personal history combines with another special context to form conceptual frameworks shared by all reporters, a context embracing the social structure and patterns of social interaction that surround journalists as they produce news. Social-interaction patterns, when added to personal histories, provide baseline reference points for the prediction of reporting on critical events.

Social Context

To suggest that social context sets a stage for reporters to write their stories is to go beyond the assertion that reporters, like their audiences, share a variety of "stereotypes," what Walter Lippman defined as "the effect of widely shared expectations in standardizing the popular perception and definition of social situations." (Lippman quoted in Roshco, 1975:112.) Bernard Roschco suggests that "these selective perceptions and rate responses inherent in stereotyping, most of them shared by journalists and much of their audiences, generate the preconceptions required for the deadline — harried choice of news content." (Roshco, 1975:112.) Such selectivity is accepted as intrinsic in news judgments made in the face of inflexible deadlines.

The social context that concerns us in this study, however, impinges more directly on reporters than does the general notion of social stereotype. Of special interest in any study of foreign correspondents is the relation between reporters and sources and the way social structure affects reporting at precisely that juncture. Reporter and scholar Bernard Roscho has written about this topic with compelling lucidity, and a number of his observations merit summary.

For Roshco, a strong system of what Herbert Gans calls a "mutual obligation system" between reporter and source evolves in a complex way. That system implies more than a reporter's inevitable acquisition of "guilty knowledge." It suggests more than the immediate benefits of "inside" access to unattributable stories. Rather, the patterned reciprocity of source-reporter relations is tied to evolving "working arrangements" between sources and the newsmen on their "beat."

This working relationship may produce not only selective coverage based on shared likes and dislikes, but also a shared "identity." Referring to local news coverage, for example, Gans suggests that "over time the (beat) reporter becomes a part of political institutions, if only marginally, and his coverage begins to be selective, sometimes deliberately, but more often unconsciously. Getting to know his major news sources well, he forms likes and dislikes which cannot help but influence his reporting." (Herbert Gans in Roshco, 1975: 113.) In addition, since the beat reporter is likely to spend

much of his working time with his regular sources, he begins to "identify" in-
evitably to some extent with these "colleagues." (Roschko, 1975:114.) *New
York Times* reporter and humorist Russell Baker expresses the consequences
of the "identity" process this way:

> The capitol reporter . . . affects the hooded expression of the man privy to
> many important deals. The Pentagon man always seems to have just come in off
> maneuvers. The State Department reporter quickly learns to talk like a fuddy-
> duddy — and to look grave, important and inscrutable. (Russell Baker quoted in
> Roshco, 1975:114.)

Through the evolution of comfortable working relationships, news
"selection" and "identification" occur, at least to some extent, and sources
are likely to become what sociologists like to call an "alternative reference
group." The routines of journalism practice may often produce shared
reporter-official perspectives on events. To be certain, conflict may occur,
and one of the purposes of this study is to investigate the likelihood of
reporter-source conflict. Whatever the probabilities of disagreement, powerful constraints inherent in the structure of reporting careers encourage journalists and close sources to share a vast domain of common perspectives on
political and social change. In foreign affairs reporting, a journalist covering
the State Department or Pentagon, or a correspondent relying often on U.S.
Foreign Service or U.S. military personnel abroad for stories, all establish
reciprocal information networks with sources.

How do personal histories of journalists and the social structure of
reporting mesh to form professional perspectives on foreign affairs journalism? What process describes their interactions?

In order to chart the way reporters acquire perspectives on professionalism in journalism and ultimately on crisis reporting, it is useful to
regard the process as one of learning or socialization. A socialization approach focuses on the factors or agents that affect individual learning and
compares their relative strength. In this study, we are concerned with
discovering the agents that affect the formation of journalists' perspectives
on professional reporting. What socialization models are available for comparison? What attitude components or clusters best define "professional"
perspectives on journalism? What array of socialization agents can we select
in order to weigh their relative importance in predicting professional orientations toward foreign affairs reporting?

Three Learning Models

To sort the ways prior experience and social contexts affect crisis reporting,
it is useful to construct some distinct paths journalists possibly take in their
initiation and maturity as foreign affairs reporters. These learning paths are

presented here as simple, descriptive models, any one of which might illustrate the proces of becoming a foreign correspondent. Such models are abstract, but they reveal general background patterns that furnish a context for more specific learning about appropriate attitudes toward reporting as a profession, foreign policy officials, and East-West strategies.

Cumulative Learning

The first learning model is essentially a "classic" perspective that assumes, as a point of departure, that most significant learning is essentially cumulative. It may be considered rather incremental, one stage following another, as in the work of Piaget. Or it may be full of drama and crisis, as in the Oedipal and adolescent crises emphasized by Freud. What they and other learning theorists often share, however, is a belief that important learning is a building process in which later knowledge is grafted onto a core of earlier learning.

This cumulative perspective has been applied to the learning of social attitudes by many students of political attitude formation. Some emphasize the importance of personality in predicting attitudes (Greenstein, 1969), while others suggest that families exert profound influence. (Davies, 1965; Langton, 1969.) Still others point to early schooling as a key source of political and social attitudes. (Hess and Torney, 1967.)

Whatever the learning, or "socialization," agent illuminated by various studies, virtually all seem to share an underlying premise: that political learning is cumulative. What one learns later in life is integrated into what one has already learned in the process of personality formation, in the family or in early schooling.

In the case of foreign affairs reporting, cumulative learning would envision acquiring perspectives on professional reporting through early learning, perhaps during adolescence or during formative, initial stages of a career enmeshed in foreign-policy issues, with later learning grafted onto earlier experience in a relatively smooth progression. A cumulative learning path might be used to describe the changes undergone by reporters, who, through questions arising from the Bay of Pigs, the Dominican Republic intervention of 1965, and Vietnam, gradually reinterpreted views about U.S. foreign policy and about social change in the Third World prevalent immediately after World War II.

Contained Learning

Learning political and social attitudes, however, may sometimes fail to occur so smoothly. Two other learning models can be forwarded in an effort to describe the possible socialization paths traveled by foreign-affairs reporters. One model refers to "contained" learning. In this process, socially relevant learning is telescoped into a short time frame: an individual learns almost all he needs to know professionally within a short time space at a relatively young age, and that learning is reinforced throughout the remainder of his professional life. The structure of "contained" learning is characterized by congruence of early and later learning. Applied to foreign affairs journalists, those who continue after Vietnam to think about their professional roles, relations with officials, and Cold War maxims in the same way they viewed such things immediately after World War II might be said to display "contained" learning about journalism and foreign policy. Early learning foreshadows later learning identically.

Contained learning is far more rigid than the gradual accumulation of new roles and attitudes. Yet it refers to only one kind of departure from the incrementalism of the cumulative model. Learning social attitudes, rather than proceeding smoothly through some process of addition, or through the petrified reinforcement of contained perspectives acquired early in life, may occur through abrupt dislocations and sharp disjunctures. A third model of learning calls attention to those disjunctures, postulating that they may be present in social learning and significant in answering questions about adult behavior.

Discontinuous Learning

Disjunctures in personal experience may be related to abrupt ruptures in political or social attitudes. Traumas of various kinds such as disease, combat experience, or national catastrophe may all be associated with disjointed or noncumulative learning.[1] Applied to the learning of professional and social attitudes by foreign-affairs reporters, the disjunctive or discontinuous path may represent the socialization experiences of those who "suddenly" began to view their country, foreign-policy officials, and their work roles differently after Vietnam (or perhaps after the Bay of Pigs or the Dominican intervention of 1965) than they had before. An abrupt shift in professional attitudes, sometimes approximating a "conversion" or "born again" euphoria, is sometimes symptomatic of the discontinuous mode of attitude acquisition.

Table I charts the distinguishing characteristics of each learning model. While the structure of the cumulative model is characterized by the *addition* of information, and the containment model by the *congruence* of early and later learning, the discontinuous model exhibits a learning structure characterized chiefly by *qualitative* or *quantum* changes in information acquisition. Another way to explain differences among the three models is to note that in cumulative learning, the socialization process involves generalization from one object to another, and in contained learning the process largely reinforces what has been learned earlier. In discontinuous learning, however, the process involves compartmentalization or specification of objects and experience. (See Table 1)

In the cumulative model, learning occurs over an extended period of time. In contained and discontinuous learning, however, learning within short time frames is significant. In the contained model, early social or career learning "contains" the expression of later attitudes. In discontinuous learning a critical experience "transforms" early learning and new learning represents a "jump" or "break" from prior learning.

These three general models of learning about political and social attitudes describe the various learning paths foreign-affairs journalists are likely to travel as they acquire professional and foreign-policy attitudes. It is possible that most may experience the smooth progression of the cumulative model. It is also possible, however, that learning may be contained more rigidly in attitude molds prefabricated immediately after World War II. Or is it possible that learning may undergo the abrupt bounces of the discontinuous perspective? Each of these general models helps guide our discussion of specific professional attitudes and the array of factors that produce them.

Definitions of Professionalism

Traditional discussions of "professionalism" in reporting emphasize, at the very least, freedom from exterior authority. "Freedom of the press" is a hallowed ideal, enshrined in the Bill of Rights. Scholars who have studied journalistic professionalism elaborate but seldom challenge that fundamental concept of freedom, "from" interference. McLeod and others, for example, have created attitude scales that suggest a professional journalist is one who: likes to express himself freely, values subject matter, may have expertise, expresses differences of opinion with the policy of his paper, emphasizes the service ideal, and may favor increased reporter participation in a news organization's policy-making. (See McLeod and Hawley, Jr., 1964:329–339, McLeod and Rush, 1969a.583–590, 1969b.784–789.) Summarizing most of the professionalism perspectives from the literature on

TABLE 1   Three Models of Learning

Element of Learning	Cumulative	Contained	Discontinuous
Structure	Addition	Congruence	Qualitative or Quantum Change
Process	Generalization	Reinforcement	Compartmentalization or Specification

occupational sociology, Oguz B. Nayman isolates four attributes of a profession: expertise, autonomy, commitment (social service), and responsibility (formalization of an occupation's ideals in a code of ethics). (Nayman, 1973:195–212.)

These studies permit comparison of journalism and other professions according to "professionalism" criteria derived from other occupations. As explained in the previous chapter, however, what "professionalism" means to working journalists may be quite different from what it means to practitioners in other occupations. For example, "expertise" may suggest obfuscation and the loss of valued fluid communication skills. "Certification" of journalists may suggest central control by outside, perhaps political, authority. Such notions are anathema to highly respected, experienced journalists.

A second objection to such definitions, in the case of political reporters, is that they provide few specific guidelines for reporting on government policies and the process of policy formation. A third objection, significant in this study of foreign affairs reporters, is that general professional frameworks furnish few guidelines for reporters engaged in reporting on social change abroad, especially in conditions of social and political crisis.

One wonders, for example, how frequently reporters for major U.S. news institutions thought about the 1973 Code of Ethics adopted by Sigma Delta Chi, the Society of Professional Journalists, when filing quick copy for tight deadlines during the struggle for power in the final months of the Shah in Iran or of the Somoza government in Nicaragua. New professional guidelines may be necessary if journalists are to incorporate some notion of "professionalism" into daily reporting on crisis and social change in the Third World. This study suggests focusing on three clusters of attitudes, encompassing attitudes toward reporting roles, toward officials, and toward strategic policy. Each of these clusters deserves discussion.

Reporter Orientations

Most reporting models that describe the social role of journalists and mass media address sets of similar polarities, or extreme cases. There are "gatekeepers," who simply select important facts from masses of detailed information, in contrast to "advocacy journalists," who strive to represent the viewpoints and interests of competing groups, especially those of excluded and underprivileged groups. (White, 1950:383–90; Janowitz, 1975:618–626.) Others contrast "neutral" reporting roles with "participant" ones. These terms are used by Wiseberger and Johnstone, *et al.* to describe professional reporting orientations in domestic reporting, and by Cohen and Batscha to refer to distinct policy roles performed by foreign affairs journalists. (Weisberg, 1961; Johnstone, Slawski, and Bowman, 1976: Chapt. 7; Cohen, 1963:Chapt. 2; Batascha, 1975:Chapt. 2.)

Each of these polarities is useful in expressing opposing viewpoints about appropriate roles for journalists. As presented however, the dualities of gatekeeper and advocate, or "neutral" observer and "participant," are too ambiguous to be useful in a careful analysis of reporting roles linked to newspaper performance. Such terms represent less a set of analytical categories than diametrically opposed positions in an occupational and perhaps generational debate about appropriate professional utopias for the craft of journalism. This study suggests use of the terms "chronicler" and "examiner" to represent the two positions, terms derived from names of functioning newspapers. A "chronicler" perspective would refer to breadth, restraint, and "technically efficient" journalism, while an "examiner" perspective would emphasize "investigative, analytic, and interpretive reporting," (Johnstone, *et al.,* 1976:114, 116.)

The terms "chronicler" and "examiner" display several advantages for careful researchers. The neutral-participant dichotomy suggests that one role is extremely passive, the other extremely active. Given these choices, a reader is tempted to assume that almost every media institution might fall into some version of the "participant" category, since the absolute "neutrality" of newspapers, privately owned but performing public functions (and therefore serving as public institutions) is difficult to imagine. The categories of neutral and participant therefore shrink one category and fatten another so much that readers and social scientists are deprived of useful analytical constructs. The suggested categories of "chronicler" and "examiner," by contrast, recognize that all newspapers are in some sense social participants, playing visible social roles.[2]

"Chronicler" and "examiner" are also superior to "gatekeeper" and "advocate." "Gatekeeper," like the word "participant," is a category so large among professional journalists that almost everyone can belong to it. "Advocate," by contrast, suggests a rather small group of journalists championing the interests of groups with little regularized access to the media. (See Janowitz, *op.cit.*). The "examiner" model, although it contains aspects of the advocacy category, is far broader and carries a more profound sense of judicious deliberation than does the concept of "advocate." "Chronicler" and "examiner" are used in this study to signify an important professional choice confronting journalists, in this case foreign-affairs reporters. Two other major orientations are also significant in evaluating the professional perspectives of foreign-affairs reporters.

For the purposes of this study, an "examiner" orientation will be defined as more "professional" than a "chronicler" perspective. Although both orientations may be considered professional by some journalists, an examining journalist is more likely: to display a broader historical and social perspective on daily events and to exhibit relatively greater autonomy from a deadline mentality, which emphasizes speed, breadth, and accuracy. In practice, a journalist may be compelled to display a substantial concern with speed, breadth, and accuracy in order to remain employed. Behavior apart, however, a correspondent who demonstrates a consistent *attitudinal preference* for historical examination or in-depth analysis of events as an occupational ideal is considered highly professional under conditions of crisis.

Official Orientations

A hallmark of professional reporting is a concern for freedom of the press, defined as "autonomy" from official interference. That concern may be expressed in a creed that implies a "distancing" of journalists from "external" interests and a fidelity to the internally generated norms of the journalism profession. Creeds promoting this kind of insulation may be composed of such elements as: belief in the primacy of service to audience or readership (over and above any duties owed to organized political authority); emphasis on the need to master certain specialist communication skills before audiences can be addressed effectively; and a belief in the "watchdog" function of journalism and the need for media to adopt an adversary stance. (Blumler and Gurevitch, 1975:165-193.)

Focussing on foreign affairs reporters, those who display "distancing" or "autonomous" orientations concerning relations with officials may hold a number of attitudes. They may be likely to verify carefully information received from unauthorized sources in the U.S. State Department prior to publication. They may work rather independently of Department information officers. They may bring public views and needs to the attention of State Department officers. And they may complement Department press releases with independent opinions about the same information. Finally, "distanced" journalists may tend to view relations between reporters and officials in either Washington, D.C., or the field to be somewhat more adversarial than collegial. Each of these characteristics helps define an attitude cluster held by relatively autonomous journalists.

Strategic Orientations

A final attitude dimension can be included in the array of professional orientations associated with foreign affairs journalism. A concern with accurately reporting indicators of social change in the Third World implies a sensitivity to the internal social, economic, and political problems found in each country. An appreciation of the indigenous aspects of social change may be blunted if it is overbalanced by a concern for international strategic issues. Stated simply, a fixation on the East-West implications of crises in the Third World may dull the ability of journalists (as well as officials) to anchor their perceptions in the serious internal inequalities that can generate social conflict.

In this analysis, an orientation that appreciates internal inequalities in the Third World is assumed somewhat at variance with one that generally engages in what former Secretary of State Henry Kissinger calls "linkage." Those who see East-West security issues as inherent in every internal conflict in the Third World or in every North-South debate are seldom likely to grant presumptive legitimacy to those calling for change. It can be assumed, therefore, that those displaying attitudes that consider appropriate U.S. intervention generally, or conflict with the Soviet Union or "communism" specifically, are diminished in their receptivity to change in the Third World. Conversely, those who more consistently favor non-intervention generally and detente specifically are assumed more sensitive to the legitimacy of change in the Third World.

Taken together, the reporting, official, and strategic orientations of journalists help define an ideal vision of "professional" reporting on social change in foreign affairs. Those who display reporting attitudes favoring the "examiner" perspective, who cherish "autonomy" from officials and who generally favor non-intervention and East-West detente, are judged highly "professional" in reporting on social change abroad. Conversely, those whose attitudes favor the "chronicler" perspective on reporting, cherish close contacts with officials, and customarily favor intervention generaly and conflict with the Soviet Union specifically, will be judged in this study as less professional in reporting on crises and social change abroad.

Five warnings are necessary at this juncture. First, the three definitions of professionalism offered for discussion represent a special perspective on profesional reporting. Other definitions of professionalism may be useful at different times. This study simply suggests that under crisis conditions, an orientation favoring an "examiner" perspective toward reporting, an adversarial perspective toward officials, and a non-intervention perspective toward East-West conflict is a model of professional excellence.

A second caution is that although a "professional" foreign affairs reporter is defined in multi-dimensional terms, no argument is advanced that at this juncture that these dimensions necessarily cohere in some obvious way. They may all be highly related, but that will be tested elsewhere. At this point, professional foreign affairs reporting is simply "defined" as demonstrating relative tendencies toward "examiner" attitudes more than toward others, relative tendencies toward adversarial attitudes more than others, and so forth.

A third caution is that an orientation favoring non-intervention, tolerance of national differences, and plural choices in international affairs does not necessarily represent endorsement of a specific administration's East-West policies. To call a reporting orientation favoring "detente" professional is not to claim that a professional reporter should automatically approve a foreign policy that promotes what particular state department representatives or elected officials call "detente." In this study, detente simply refers to a general disposition tolerating many national options in international affairs, along with a general preference for non-intervention. The detente orientation is explained more fully in Chapter VI.)

Fourth, these ideal and non ideal visions of professional reporting are extreme cases. Most journalists doubtless fall between the extremes in their professional preferences. But these ideal types do define dimensions along which journalists can be compared, judging some as more professional than others.

Fifth, to define a collection of reporting perspectives as a "professional orientation toward social change" is not to make judgments about the desirability of different kinds of social change in specific instances. Our immediate concern is not with the approval or disapproval of social change, but rather with reporting perspectives that examine and explore seriously claims made about inequality and the need for change. Nevertheless, throughout this study it will be assumed that a "professional" reporter is one who stresses issue reexamination, autonomy from outside influences, and respect for national differences, and therefore considers major efforts at social change worthy of serious examination.

The Learning "Transfer" Hypothesis: Explanatory Factors

Prior experience and social context are assumed to be associated with the formation of professional orientations towards foreign affairs reporting. Tracing the impact of these experiences, pre-crisis learning is divided into three factors: occupational experience, pre-occupational experience, and informal social networks.

Three Sources of Learning

Occupational Experience
A sizeable number of studies regard news institutions and occupational experience as essential shapers of reporting perspectives. Such studies typically consider some of the following occupational factors as significant: number of years spent in journalism, number of organizations served, salary level, organizational rank, time devoted to managerial tasks, degree of supervision, and degree of cooperation with work associates. Several authors have studied the impact of these factors on American reporters, for example, Leon Sigal (1973), Edward J. Epstein (1973), and — with modern survey

research methods — Johnstone, Slawski, and Bowman, (1976). Regarding foreign affairs reporting in particular, Cohen (1963) and Batscha (1975) illuminate the constraints occupational contexts place on the daily routines of foreign affairs journalists.

Although a great deal is known about the influence of work context on reporting perspectives, little attention has been paid to the impact of pre-occupational experiences and informal social networks on the professional attitudes of reporters. Personal, pre-occupational experiences, of course, are considered important by psychologists in studying personality formation. Scholars interested in political socialization, in the influence of early learning on adult political and social attitudes, have documented the way personal, pre-occupational experiences affect adult political values generally (see R. Siegal 1965; S. Schwartz 1975; N. Cutler, 1975; J. Pollock, 1975). But little is known about the way early experiences affect the professional perspectives of reporters.

Pre-occupational Experience
Those who believe that perspectives on journalistic autonomy and pluralist reporting are formed relatively early in life might focus on pre-occupational factors such as level of education, prestige of college attended (if any), size of city of origin, military experience, year of graduation, and year of birth. Even sibling number and birth order may be significant in the acquisition of adult professional orientations. Such factors are standard variables used to study attitude formation in research on value acquisition and political socialization.

Informal Social Networks
In addition to pre-occupational experience, the influence of another area of pre-crisis experience has also been given little attention by researchers interested in learning how reporters acquire attitudes towards their vocation. Anthropologists believe that informal social networks can exert a gigantic influence on adult attitudes. In parallel fashion, researchers sensitive to anthropological thinking might suspect that social networks are potentially quite significant in predicting journalists' attitudes, especially under conditions of crisis. They might expect the following factors to assume importance: degree of informal contact with other journalists or with officials and executives, professional memberships, degree of "craft" as opposed to organizational identification, social proximity to sources, and friendships with nationals of the host country where a reporter is posted. Each of these factors — occupational, pre-occupational, and informal — may be associated with two distinct learning mechanisms.

Two Modes of Learning

One mechanism can be called "identification." This learning procedure expects that the individual will acquire attitudes by imitating some significant other person — a parent, a teacher, or in this case, more experienced reporters or editors. In this mode of learning, attitudes toward a given person or group may be acquired by direct imitation of a respected role model. Those who believe that occupational experiences are the primary influences affecting a reporter's view of his profession are likely to consider the "identification" learning mechanism important. They may believe that what correspondents learn about professional reporting is acquired primarily by the direct imitation of journalists with whom an individual interacts or whom the individual admires.

But a second learning mechanism is possible: interpersonal transfer or diffusion. The "transfer" learning procedure assumes that in his relations with adults, an individual may establish "modes of interaction" which are similar to those he established with persons in his earlier, pre-adult experience. (Harrington, 1970:9.) Another possibility in transferred learning is that journalists will establish patterns of interaction which are similar to those they experience with persons in informal social situations. The transfer learning mechanism expects that attitudes developed toward one person are transferred to apply to a new object or set of persons. Direct imitation of someone else does not occur, because the learning is indirect and "transferred" from one situation to a new, distinct situation.

Occupational Factors

To test the relative importance of the identification and transfer modes of learning, several specific hypothesis can be formulated. A core assumption guides these hypotheses. It is that the more "privileged" an individual is in his work (or for that matter, in his pre-occupational experience and informal social networks) the more likely he is to be or believe he is an "autonomous" individual, highly self-reliant, requiring few external cues to direct him, and resistant to those who would dissuade him from his chosen course. This study assumes that privilege or the feeling of privilege is associated with an admiration for journalistic autonomy, expressed in the following ways: freedom to examine thoroughly the social and political implications of a given issue; freedom to resist inappropriate pressure exerted by officials; and freedom to examine events in each country on their own terms, independent of their implications for East-West conflict or cooperation. Expressing this hypothesis succinctly, the richer an occupational journalist's experience — whether expressed in journalistic longevity, status, travel, salary, or sense of community with associates at work — the more likely he is to acquire autonomous "professional" perspectives.

The learning mechanism in this case is possibly one of identification. Those who have achieved a great deal in their careers as journalists can acquire professional attitudes by direct imitation of other respected colleagues. Those who consider themselves relatively advantaged or privileged by the news institutions employing them or who exhibit a strong sense of community with superiors and subordinates are presumed likely to display a high regard for the hallmark of a dedicated reporter: an admiration for an "autonomous" professional orientation.

Preoccupational Factors

As with occupational privilege, it is also assumed that the more privileged an individual is in his early experiences, the more likely he is to exhibit autonomous professional perspectives as an adult. Unlike direct learning by imitation (likely in explaining the impact of occupational factors on professional perspectives), the learning mechanism in this case is likely to be interpersonal transfer or diffusion. Early privilege may become translated into adult orientations admiring independence and autonomy generally, and professional reporting in particular.

Early privilege may be manifested in many years of formal schooling, enrollment in or graduation from a prestige school, and military experience (providing opportunities to view alternative lifestyles). Some scholars also suggest that aspects of early *family* experience, in particular birth-order and sibling number, also contribute significantly to adult perspectives on politics and society. Such factors may also assume importance in predicting adult attitudes toward occupations.

An individual's family of origin can be quite important, not only in its impact on personality, but also in its influence on adult political and social orientations. Kenneth Langton (1969), for example, concludes that the family (specifically its level of interest in politics) is the most potent predictor of an indiviual's adult sense of political efficacy or self-confidence. Langton arrived at this conclusion by comparing the impact of family with the impact of peer groups and schooling on individual political attitudes. (Langton, 1969:159–159, 173–174.) In a related study of the learning patterns of elite government officials in a South American country, John Pollock concluded that officials from relatively large families tend to exhibit a relatively high level of empathy with others and to feel responsible for others, particularly for low-income citizens. (Pollock, 1973b; 1975b.) The Pollock investigation indicates that the family as an agent of socialization enjoys a remarkable staying power, influencing perceptions of: individual political mobility, job mobility, and merit recruitment in government.

Number of siblings aside, some scholarly evidence also suggests that first-born (and only children) are somewhat different from others in their social and political attitudes. The findings are somewhat contradictory. Some scholars suggest that first born and singleton children tend to be responsible and high achievers, but they also tend to be less empathic and exhibit less esteem — if in multi-sibling families — than later born children. (Stotland and Cottrell, 1962; 183–91; Stotland and Dunn, 1963: 532–540; Dittes and Capra, 1962: 329–335; Renshon in Schwartz, 1975: 69–95.) Other scholars suggest that first-born children are generally found to be more insecure than later arrivals. (Sears, Macoby, and Levin, 1957.) Despite the studies suggesting that first-born children are somewhat disadvantaged, a recently published, thorough review of survey research over the past few decades suggests two contrary findings:

1. First-born children, to the extent that they are at all different from later born children, tend to be relatively happy and relatively satisfied with important aspects of life, notably jobs and health.
2. More important than emphasizing differences between only children or first-born children and others is a broader comparison, specifically, comparing children from small families (including only children) with those from large families. (Blake, 1981: 43–54.)

The researcher concludes that family size, specifically the number of siblings a respondent has, is more important than an individual's birth order in influencing adult social attitudes (Blake 1981: 43–54). Whatever their areas of agreement or disagreement, a number of scholars have found that early sibling experience has a significant impact on adult attitudes. Several studies suggest that individuals from relatively large families are likely to be more secure than individuals from small families. (Bossard and Bowl, 1956; Clausen, 1968; Renshon, 1975.) In turn, early security may encourage adult autonomy, generally, and perhaps professional autonomy specifically. It is likely that family size affects adult professional reporting perspectives.

Family size apart, an individual's age may be linked to adult autonomy. Although age in itself is not a factor that occurs prior to occupational experience, it stands apart from that experience. Age *per se* is also assumed associated with multiple opportunities for privilege, for experiencing alternative possibilities and for empathy and therefore is initially presumed linked to a potential for professional, autonomous reporting.

Year of graduation from college or year reporting work was begun, both of which help measure generational differences may be more closely associated with professional prospectives than age *per se*. Those who have graduated or began work relatively long ago, closer in time to World War II than to the 1960s, are likely to hold a different set of social and political perspectives than those who have entered full-time occupations in more recent years. Taken together, schooling, family (and in particular sibling) experience, age, and historical generation constitute pre-occupational or extra-occupational factors that can affect the professional perspectives of adult foreign affairs reporters.

Informal Social Networks

If early learning can be transferred to adult professional and social attitudes, another kind of learning can be transferred as well, from friendship patterns to beliefs about one's profession. Studies of political socialization across the life-cycle often restrict themselves to measures of occupational and pre-occupational influence. This investigation, however, endeavors to understand journalists as social beings, embedded in "informal social networks." It will be assumed that a journalist's choice of close friends has some bearing on his acquisition of professional perspectives on journalism.

To separate an individual's close associates from those who are less close is to apply concepts used frequently in sociology and anthropology. Sociologists distinguish between "primary reference groups" and "secondary" ones. Anthropologists might distinguish between relatively "bounded egocentric networks" and less bounded ones, or between an individual's "primary star" or close relationships and his "second-order star" of social relationships. (Barnes, 1968.) Whatever the terminology employed, these concepts all stress the importance of a distinction between close and more distant personal relationships.

The personal distance dimenson helps address a significant professional question: how closely can a journalist wed himself to officials, politicians and even publishers and news managers before he loses the capacity to question, think independently, and present choices, the capacity to "examine"? Presumably, to the extent journalists maintain close relations with officials, either as friends or sources, they are less likely to question official policy, less likely to examine that policy carefully, and less likely to present readers with significant policy alternatives. Close friendships can affect professional orientations.

Two specific informal factors are considered related to professional reporting perspectives: off-duty social interaction and identification with journalism as a special craft. In their survey of domestic reporters, Johnstone, et al., discovered that the higher the amount of social interaction with other colleagues in journalism, the more likely a journalist is to manifest a "participant," questioning, examining news perspective. (Johnstone, et al., 1976: Chapter 7.) Similarly, the more a journalist identifies himself as a member of a special guild, or craft, the more likely he is to be aware of or exalt what makes that profession "special."

One of the reporting profession's special qualities is autonomy: reporters can examine public assertions, weigh their veracity, and print diverse opinions. For these and other reasons, the more a journalist is integrated into the organizations and outlooks of independent journalism, the more examining or professional he may be. For example, a journalist holding many memberships in professional associations, active in such associations, and with little work experience outside journalism, may be likely to display "autonomous" examining perspectives. We can also assume that someone who is actively devoted to a craft is likely to demonstrate a highly professional orientation toward reporting on social change, transmitting and evaluating issues with respect for conflicting claims.

A final expectation about informal networks and professional reporting deserves attention, concerning field experiences. Presumably regional expertise is associated with a large number of field contacts and a relatively complex vision of the Third World. Thus, the more time a journalist has spent in the Third World, the more time spent outside capital cities, the more developed his language ability and the closer the friendships with nationals, the more likely he is to persist in examining new information. As a point of departure, this study assumes that the greater the field expertise or "field integration," the more likely a journalist is to examine official perspectives and to understand, quite apart from East-West issues, indigenous cross currents influencing social change. Learning gathered from friendship networks can be transferred to learning about professional autonomy.

Conclusion

If individual journalists are significant in affecting public views on foreign affairs, then it is useful to study the prior experiences of those journalists, along with the social contexts that surround them. To focus on the prior learning of reporters is to employ a socialization approach, suggesting that factors derived from the occupational experiences, life-cycles and social networks of reporters all exert some influence on their professional orientations toward foreign affairs journalism. This study defines professional reporting in three ways, each associated with some aspect of journalistic autonomy. It registers a preference for:

a. examination and analytical reporting more than reporting characterized by speed, breadth, and accuracy;
b. an adversarial rather than collegial posture toward officials; and
c. a tolerant pluralism in international affairs rather than a disposition toward intervention abroad or toward conflict in East-West relations.

The following chapters test which of the predictive factors is most closely associated with professional, autonomous reporting: experiences in news organizations, experiences that happen throughout the life-cycle, or informal friendship networks. Perhaps experiences close in time and association with the activity of reporting itself, in other words, organizational experiences, are critical in shaping perspectives on professional foreign affairs journalism. But perhaps pre-occupational experiences in families of origin and in higher eduation have a major, early impact on professional orientations. Or perhaps the intimate choices that manifest themselves in friendshp networks — as with pre-occupational experience, rooted in personal experience — play a major role in the formation of professional perspectives. The following chapters test which of these influence clusters is most potent in guiding the way reporters learn to become foreign correspondents.

Notes

1. For studies on the impact of disease and body image generally on political attitudes refer to Schwartz, 1973, and D. Schwartz and S.K. Schwartz, eds., 1975:96–126. The impact of combat trauma on the political views of Vietnam veterans is described in John C. Pollock, Dan White, and Frank Gold, "When Soldiers Return: Combat and Political Alienation Among White Vietnam Veterans," in Schwartz and Schwartz, 1975a:317–333. Regarding national disasters, the influence of the Kennedy assassination on children's political attitudes is investigated by Roberta S. Sigel in "An Exploration into Some Aspect of Political Socialization: School Children's Reactions to the Death of a President," in Wolfstein and Kliman, 1965:30–61.

2. What this study terms "examining" journalism is similar to what John C. Merrill calls "existential" journalism (Merrill, 1977).

PART TWO

3

Foreign Affairs Reporters
An Overview

In order to explore the questions and assumptions discussed in the two preceding chapters, it is useful to select a specific set of foreign-affairs reporters, to outline the method used to study them, and to describe their chief characteristics. These include lifecycle characteristics, organizational experience, and social-network preferences.

A Focus on Correspondents Who Have Reported on Latin America

When informed members of the public think about significant roles played by individual journalists, they often think about Vietnam. But reporting on Vietnam may be only the tip of a larger journalistic iceberg. That world may represent the clearest example of a rupture between officials and reporters, but it would be misleading to suggest that patterns of official-reporter proximity were fashioned entirely by that experience. Considered from a broad international relations perspective, our experience in Vietnam may be rather unusual.

In order to study the roles played by individual journalists in a region of long-standing concern to American foreign policy, it may be useful to examine reporters who have covered Latin America for United States news organizations. The foreign-policy context in which the Latin American correspondent and the editors who see their material operate is quite different than the context of our Indochina involvement.

First, Southeast Asia was a relatively new area of foreign policy concern for the United States, an area in which we played only an intermittent role until the mid-1950s. Second, in part because of our inexperience in the area, we seemed impelled to duplicate the historical role of the previous foreign occupants, the French, induced to fulfill the role and destiny of colonial overlords. David Halberstam expressed our position this way:

> The problem was trying to cover something everyday, when in fact, the real key was that it was all derivative of the French-Indochina War, which is history. So you really should have had a third paragraph in each story which would have said 'none of this means anything because we are in the same footsteps of the French and we are prisoners of their experience.' But given the rules of newspaper reporting you can't really do that. Events have to be judged by themselves as if the past did not really exist. This is not usually such a problem for a reporter, but to an incredible degree in Vietnam we were haunted and indeed imprisoned by the past. (D. Halberstam in a letter to P. Knightley, 1975:423.)

Finally, the proximity of Indochina, the China of Mao Zse Dong was an inescapable presence and rationale for policy, and presumably by extension, reporting.

U.S. interest in Latin America by contrast is characterized by a substantially different set of conditions. Our interest in the region is legendary, codified officially in the Monroe Doctrine of 1823 warning Europe to stay away, advising U.S. citizens of our special relationship with the Southern Hemisphere. Second, we are not prisoners of any other country's experience in the region. The Latin American independence movements of 1808–1820 to throw off Spanish control sought not to disparage, but to emulate, Washington and Jefferson. The Spanish, the Portuguese, and the British, colonial powers in the region, did not hold for Latin Americans the exhilaration or the example of the brave new experiment in independence and democracy ignited to the north of them.

Third, no major foreign power has been viewed, with the possible exception of our perceptions in the Cuban missile crisis, as capable of challenging either U.S. territory in Latin America or U.S. hegemony there. Sending U.S. troops to the Dominican Republic in 1965 was designed, according to the State Department, to prevent another Cuba of the Castro model. But that is not the same concern as anxiety over a major challenge from an incipient world power.

Each of these conditions suggests that the U.S. experience in Vietnam may have been anomalous in our history; the experience in Latin America, lasting over many decades, abundant in the varieties of foreign policies and foreign-affairs reporting displayed by the United States throughout its existence. A study of the way reporters learn to become foreign correspondents from Latin America is therefore likely to yield a cornucopia of information about the way reporters learn to become foreign correspondents in general, and how they learn to make decisions under conditions of crisis.

Latin America is not only a rich source of general reporting experience; it is also a region distinguished by critical events in which the role of U.S. journalists has been discussed and sometimes heatedly debated by scholars and journalists alike. (P. Kennedy, 1957; Barnes, 1964; G. Geyer, 1969.) Several modern examples can be listed.

The ascension to power of Fidel Castro in 1958 and 1959 and the subsequent revolution in Cuba: How did the press view Castro's origins and goals? (Zeitlin and Scheer, 1961; Lyford, 1962; M. Block, 1962; M.J. Francis, 1967; H. Matthews, 1971.)

The aborted Bay of Pigs invasion in 1961: How much did the press know and fail to release in advance of the invasion? (Bernstein and Gordon, 1967; Aronson, 1970.)

The military coup against the elected government of Jão Goulart in Brazil in 1964: How much did the U.S. press report the views of Brazil's elected government, how much the views of the generals? (Pollock and Guidette, 1980.)

The U.S. intervention in the Dominican Republic in 1965: What role did the press play in legitimizing or challenging President Johnson's justification for sending Marines to prevent a "communist" or Castro-like government takeover? (Szulc, 1965.)

The election of Dr. Salvador Allende Gossens as President of Chile in 1970 as head of a left coalition government: How much attention did the media pay to the capacity of one of Latin America's oldest democracies to elect officials of varied ideological persuasion, and how much attention was paid to instability from the right, the left, and forces outside the country itself? (Birns, 1973a, 1973b, 1973c, 1973d; P. Chain, 1973; Knudson, 1974a, 1974b, 1974c; Leggett, J.C. *et. al.,* 1978; Morris, *et. al.,* 1974; Pearson, 1973; Pollock, 1973; Pollock and Dickinson, 1974; Schakne, 1976; Pollock, 1980; Pollock and Guidette, 1980.)

These examples are mentioned not in an attempt to provide simple answers to complex questions, but rather to demonstrate that the role of the U.S. press in reporting on Latin America is a topic of surpassing interest and controversy.[1]

Method

Information on reporters who have covered Latin America for major U.S. news organizations was gathered primarily in 1978 and 1979. The available scholarly literature on foreign correspondents was reviewed in early 1978 and a questionnaire was pretested and constructed during the spring of the same year. In the course of building the questionnaire, face-to-face interviews were completed with over 40 reporters and editors who have either reported on Latin America or made gatekeeping judgments about the importance of news from that region. Most of those interviewed are employed by or have been employed by *The New York Times,* the *Washington Post,* the Associated Press, and United Press International. The questionnaire was fielded in the summers of 1978 and 1979.

Selecting an appropriate sample of correspondents concerned with Latin America was a difficult task. No convenient list exists registering the names of correspondents of major U.S. news organizations who have covered Latin America in the past and present. Since it was the intention of the study to locate as many correspondents as possible who had reported on Latin America or still cover it, it was necessary to use a "snowball" reputational sampling technique. Each of the journalists interviewed personally was asked to list as many correspondents as he or she could remember who had covered Latin American affairs for any appreciable period of time. As more and more journalists were asked to mention names, fewer and fewer new names were added to the list. All names on the final list were mentioned by at least two reporters. Two waves of questionnaires were sent to each name on the list.

To facilitate an in-depth study of journalists' life-histories, the sample was restricted to a group of reporters who had at least one characteristic in common: at some point in their careers they had or still reported on a particular world region for a major U.S. news organization. Latin America was selected as an appropriate region because it was familiar to the author and because its distance from major centers of East-West conflict permits news gatherers a relatively high amount of discretion in selecting news perspectives. Print journalists from wire services, news weeklies, and major dailies were included. Television correspondents were included only if they had a prior history of print-media reporting. Others who demonstrated considerable experience not in print reporting but in television correspondence from Latin America were found so few in number, according to the reputational referral sampling technique used in this study, that they were not included in the survey.

The final list, which included names mentioned by journalists who were contacted by mail, totaled about 134 names. The total number of respondents was 102, yielding a response rate of 76 percent. Most of the responses were obtained from questionnaires mailed to individuals who were either retired, working in a variety of locations throughout the United States, or still working in Latin America.[2]

Questionnaires were coded and the raw data processed by computer in the spring and summer of 1980. Since the response rate was unusually high, it is reasonable to assume that the results obtained in this survey can be generalized or assumed valid for the entire population of correspondents now alive who have reported on Latin America for major U.S. news organizations.

Historical and Lifecycle Factors

A cursory examination of the historical and lifecycle characteristics of the respondents considered altogether yields the following observations:

Most reporters entered the work force during a historical period of substantial East-West conflict.

Whether through early or later family experiences, a substantial portion of the journalists in this study have been exposed to lessons in self-reliance.

As a group, correspondents are rather well-educated. A sizable proportion of them have attended some of the best universities in the United States.

A substantial proportion of correspondents, 45 percent of those who attended college, attended universities on the East Coast either in New England or within the states that lie within the New York-Washington, D.C., corridor.

Exposure to East-West Conflict

The journalists identified in this study belong to a wide range of age categories. About somewhere near a third are 40 or younger or 51 or older, and almost another third are concentrated between the ages 41 and 50.

Despite their broad age distribution, it is important to note that most of the correspondents entered adulthood during periods of substantial East-West conflict. About 44 percent of the correspondents who graduated from college received their degrees prior to the summer of 1957, when the Soviet satellite "Sputnik" was launched. Another 38 percent of the respondents who received college degrees graduated between 1957 and 1967, between Sputnik and the Tet Offensive in Vietnam in the early spring of 1968. The remainder, 18 percent, graduated more recently: after the Tet Offensive, or since 1968. About 85 percent of the correspondents who received college degrees graduated prior to the Tet Offensive in Vietnam, prior to major shifts in thinking about East-West conflict (see Table 2).

In parallel fashion, most journalists began reporting on Latin America prior to a massive reexamination of foreign-policy strategy among both policy-makers and journalists. About three out of ten (27 percent) began reporting on Latin America prior to 1958, prior to Sputnik; about four out of ten (39 percent) began reporting between Sputnik and Tet, between 1958 and 1967. Only about one-third (34 percent) began reporting from 1968 onward, after the Tet Offensive. Considering the distribution of their ages, the years most of them graduated from college, and the years most correspondents began reporting on Latin America, it is clear that the vast majority of them began their adult careers as journalists during a period when East-West conflict was embedded in the perceptual landscape of policy-makers and journalists alike.

Consistent with the period they graduated from college and began reporting on Latin America, a little over half of the journalists have served in the Armed Forces of the United States, 6 percent in the Reserves and 50 percent on active duty. A substantial proportion of the journalists who became foreign correspondents have more than vicarious experience with World War II, the Korean War, the war in Vietnam and the draft that followed World War II.

Of the 50 percent of the sample on active duty, a little over half (27 per-

TABLE 2

	Age	
	%*	Cumulative %
40 or less	36	36
41 – 50	28	65
51 or More	35	100
	(102)**	

	Year Received College Degree		
	%	Adjusted %	Cumulative %
No degree	15	0	0
Pre-Sputnik	38	44	44
(June, 1957, prior to summer)			
Pre Tet Offensive	32	38	82
(June, 1967, prior to winter 1968)			
Post Tet Offensive	15	18	100
(Since 1968)	(102)	(87)	

*Total may not add to 100% due to rounding
**All numbers in parenthesis in this and other tables are absolute numbers. The absolute
  number typically refers to the column total.

cent of the total) have served one or two years in the service, while a little less than half (about 23 percent of the total) have served more years. Each of the preceding factors may have contributed to the perception of East-West conflict as an "almost natural" element of thinking about international affairs in general and U.S. foreign policy in particular (see Table 3).

Personal and Lifecycle Factors

Two aspects of the personal lives of Latin American correspondents are noteworthy and may contribute to later thinking about foreign-affairs reporting. One characteristic journalists exhibit is that a large portion of them have been exposed to experiences fostering self-reliance. A second characteristic of journalists is that they are well-educated, and many of them received their undergraduate educations in the Eastern portion of the United States.

Lessons in Self-Reliance

Whether through early or late family experience, a sizable number of Latin American correspondents have been compelled to be self-reliant. About half the respondents (49 percent) are first born; about 34 percent are the second children in their families. This early birth order contributes to self-reliance in several ways: parents expect a great deal of their first child, in part because they have so little experience as parents. Second, because they have no or few siblings for allies, first-born children typically rely on their parents' expectations for guidance; they have few defenses against the wishes of their

TABLE 3

| | Year Began Reporting on Latin America | |
	%	Cumulative %
Pre Sputnik	27	27
Pre Tet Offensive	39	66
Post Tet Offensive	34	100
	(100)	

| | Military Experience | |
	%	Cumulative %
None	44	44
Reserves	6	50
One or Two Years	27	77
More than Two Years	23	100
	(102)	

parents. Third, in order to meet those expectations, first-born children are notoriously apt to be both anxious and "overachievers," highly ambitious. (See Renshon, 1975:69–75). Birth order aside, self-reliance is encouraged because most respondents come from families of three or few children.

Similar lessons in adult self-reliance have been learned by about three out of ten respondents. About 11 percent have always been single and another 18 percent have been divorced. Most of those, 13 percent, have remarried. Curiously, no correspondent reported having been widowed. Whether through being single or being divorced, 29 percent of the respondents have undergone experiences that compel self-reliance (see Table 4).

High Levels of Education

Whether we examine number of years of college completed, proportion of Masters degrees earned, or prestige of colleges attended, the foreign correspondents surveyed in this study can be considered well-educated. About half of the total, 48 percent, have only four years of college experience; another two out of ten (22 percent) have completed five years of college, and yet another two out of ten (20 percent) have completed six or seven years of

TABLE 4

| | Birth Order | |
	%	Cumulative %
First-born	49	49
Second-born	34	73
Later born	17	100
	(102)	

| | Total Sibling Number | |
	%	Cumulative %*
Only Child	12	12
One Sibling	32	44
Two	26	70
Three or more	29	99
	(102)	

| | Marital Status | |
	%	Cumulative %*
Married to Original Spouse	69	69
Remarried	13	82
Divorced	5	87
Single	11	98
Other	3	101
	(102)	

*Does not add to 100 due to rounding

college. Only two respondents have no college experience, and only 10 percent of those who enrolled failed to complete four years.

Of those with B.A. degrees, only about one-fourth (26 percent) majored in journalism; about one-third (33 percent) majored in the humanities; and about two out of ten (22 percent) majored in social sciences. About a quarter (25 percent of the sample) have Masters degrees; half of that group received a Masters in journalism. Regarding status of educational institutions attended, about half (52 percent) went to well-known universities; 34 percent attended elite private universities; and 18 percent attended state universities. The diversity of their majors and the quality of their educational institutions suggest that the correspondents are an intellectually curious, well-educated group[3] (see Table 5).

Those with the highest degrees, those with M.A.s (and one Ph.D.), tend to be the youngest people in the sample. Of those with degrees, among respondents 40 or younger, 39 percent have M.A.s, whereas among those in

TABLE 5

	College Major		
	%	Adjusted %	Cumulative %
Social Sciences (and 3% Natural Sciences)	22	29	27
Humanities	33	41	68
Journalism	26	32	100
Other	5	0	
No College	14	0	____
	(102)	(83)	

	Highest Degree		
	%		
B.A.	75		
M.A. (plus one Ph.D.)	25		
No Degree	0		
	(87)		

	Status of Undergraduate College*	
	%	Cumulative %
Elite	34	34
State University	18	52
Other	48	100
No College	0	____
	(88)	

*The relative status of colleges and universities, because they change slowly, are estimated by referring to a current guide: James Cass and Max Birnbaum, Comparative Guide to American Colleges, N.Y.: Harper and Row, 1979.

their 40s, only 12 percent have M.A.s; of those 51 or older, only 20 percent have M.A.s. Similarly, the younger group reports more years of schooling. Among those respondents 40 years old or younger, 54 percent have five or more years of schooling, whereas only 46 percent of those in their 40s have five or more years; only 26 percent who are 51 or above have a similar amount of schooling.

Regional Experience

About 45 percent of the respondents received bachelor's degrees in the Eastern United States. About 26 percent went to college in the Middle Atlantic states, often along the New York-Washington corridor, while about 19 percent attended college in New England. About two out of ten (21 percent) attended college in the North Central states, 18 percent in the South, and 16 percent in West and Southwest. About 12 percent did not complete college at all.

Organizational Experience

The Career Structure of Foreign-Affairs Reporters

Compared to other professions, journalism is often considered to be an occupation that values, or at least tolerates, idiosyncrasies and individual differences. The prevailing view of journalism is that the work is often "non-routine," producing a special bureaucracy in which the hierarchy may be shallow; the occupation is compartmentalized into a wide range of expected tasks likely to change from one workplace to another; the number of "exceptional cases" or situations encountered in the "non-routine" work is large; and the "search process' is not particularly regularized (logical , systematic, or analytical). (Tunstall, 1972). The journalists encountered in this study manifest several of the characteristics of this view of journalism as a "non-routine" profession, but reporters who have covered Latin America for major U.S. papers also display a substantial amount of stability and regard for teamwork in their career descriptions.

There is certainly some awareness of hierarchy in that most journalists describe their field experience in Latin America as devoted more to reporting than to managing, whereas the same journalists report that a majority of their time in the United States is devoted to operations other than reporting (to managing and editing). Consistent with this awareness of hierarchy, almost half (about 44 percent) believe their supervisors exert considerable, or (in 4 percent of the cases) strong, control over them. The other 56 percent believe that their supervisors exert little or no control over them. Taken as a group, correspondents are somewhat ambivalent regarding their autonomy from close supervision.

The correspondents studied in this analysis, nevertheless, demonstrate similarities with their colleagues elsewhere in journalism. Most respondents have authority over relatively few employees. Five out of ten say they have authority over no other employees, and another 24 percent say they have authority over only one to five employees. These findings are consistent with descriptions of the reporting profession in general, that it is characterized by a relatively shallow hierarchy in which few people exercise a great deal of authority over others. Few correspondents appear to wield substantial authority over a large number of other employees. Seven out of ten report that they have substantially less than large or ultimate power over hiring and firing.

The journalists encountered in the study also demonstrate a wide range of salaries. Their income categories span a wide range of categories. About seven out of ten of the journalists in this study register highest salaries of less than $37,500. These estimates are consistent with the view of journalists generally, as well as correspondents in particular, as professionals who, for all their skill and prestige, are not highly paid, nor are they given considerable authority over other employees (see Table 6).

Yet a special caution is necessary. For all their "non-routine," characteristics, and however much they may appear to be relatively independent professionals, correspondents analyzed in this study believe they engage in a substantial amount of teamwork and display a remarkable amount of stability in their careers. Half of the respondents believe that most of their work involves a substantial amount of teamwork, and another 18 percent believe at least half of their work involves team efforts. This finding suggests that almost seven out of ten who have reported on Latin America think of themselves as involved in team efforts a substantial portion of the time.

In addition, most respondents have worked for a single organization for a long time. Only about one-third (34 percent) have worked ten or fewer years for the same organization. Another third have worked between eleven and seventeen years for the same organization, and yet another third (32 percent) have worked more than eighteen years for the same organization. Adding the last two categories, it is clear that about two-thirds of the correspondents (66 percent) have worked for the same organization eleven years or more. In both their descriptions of the amount of teamwork they experience and in the long tenure of their positions at a single organization, most correspondents believe that they are not simply individuals operating autonomously. Rather, they are integrated into relatively long-term collegial and organizational environments (see Table 7).

TABLE 6

Degree of Supervisor Control	%	Cumulative %
Strong	4	4
Considerable	40	44
Little	32	76
None	24	100
	(100)	

Number of Employees who Report to Respondent	%	Cumulative %
None	50	50
1–5	24	74
More than 5	26	100
	(95)	

Self-Reported Influence Over Hiring and Firing	%	Cumulative %*
None	43	43
Little	12	55
Moderate	15	70
Large	18	88
Ultimate	13	101
	(94)	

Highest Earned Annual Salary ($)	%	Cumulative %
Less than 20,000	14	14
20,001 – 27,499	21	35
27,500 – 37,499	35	70
37,500 – 44,999	16	86
45,000 or More	14	100
	(101)	

*Exceeds 100% due to rounding

TABLE 7

| | Perceived Amount of Teamwork Encountered | |
	%	Cumulative %*
Mostly Operate as an Individual	32	32
Half Individual, Half Teamwork	19	51
Mostly Teamwork	50	101
	(97)	

| | Longest Number of Years Worked for a Single News Organization | |
	%	Cumulative %
10 or Fewer	34.3	34.3
11 – 17	33.3	68
18 or More	32	100
	(102)	

*Total adds to more than 100% due to rounding

Institutional Structure and Performance

Traditional foreign affairs journalists, of course, do not inhabit some abstract, non-specific career space. They belong to concrete news organizations and, as may be expected, form judgments about the performance of those news organizations in reporting on Latin America.

Organizations As Employers

The traditional view of foreign-affairs reporters is that they are relatively "special" journalists with relatively high autonomy, a broad range of topics to cover, and a wide range of sources. It is often assumed that their work has little demonstrable relation to either advertising or paper-selling revenue goals. (Tunstall, 1972.) To be sure, foreign affairs reporters may enjoy more autonomy than their domestic counterparts, but the autonomy of the organizations they work for may be subject to obvious constraints.

About 45 percent of the respondents in this study have worked a long time for the Associated Press or United Press International, wire services with an interest in selling news to the broadest possible range of newspapers and the broadest possible public. It is possible that the efforts of these services and agencies to distribute or sell news to the broadest possible public may reduce somewhat the autonomy of both organizations and the correspondents they employ. If the marketplace for such organizations is defined as national in scope, both news institutions and their journalists may in some way be wary of straying very far from either conventional wisdom or a contemporary consensus on appropriate views of international affairs and

U.S. foreign policy. The larger the marketplace for news, the more diverse the range of opinions one is likely to encounter, and, correspondingly, the less likely organizations or reporters are to deviate substantially from a broad consensus of domestic opinion.

By contrast, news organizations (and their employees) who are less directly connected to the production of immense quantities of news, or to the distribution of news to the broadest public, enjoy more opportunities for taking positions somewhat at variance with either official or public opinion. These organizations include the major news weeklies (*Time, Newsweek, U.S. News & World Report,* and *Business Week*), other major newspapers (for example, the *Los Angeles Times,* the *Miami Herald,* the *Wall Street Journal,* and the *Christian Science Monitor*), and the *Washington Post* and *The New York Times.* Thirty-five percent of the sample has worked a long time for either the news weeklies or newspapers mentioned, excluding the last two papers. And about 21 percent of the respondents have worked a long time for *The New York Times* or the *Washington Post.* (It should be noted that the youngest correspondents work at the news organizations connected with news services. Among those 40 or younger, 78 percent work for news-service related organizations. Among those in their 40s, 62 percent do so, and among those 51 years of age or more, only 56 percent do so) (see Table 8).

TABLE 8

	Organizations Where Respondents Have Worked Longest	
	%	Cumulative %*
Associated Press	25.5	25.5
United Press	19.6	45
Several Major Daily Papers (Christian Science Montitor; Los Angeles Times; Maimi Herald; Wall Street Journal)	18	63
Major News Weeklies	16.7	79.7
The New York Times; The Washington Post	20.6	100.13
	(102)	

	Different Target News Audiences %
Broad Market (Wire Services)	45
Select Market (Others)	55
	(102)

*Total Exceeds 100% due to rounding

Journalists may evaluate the performance of the organizations they work for in several ways. Two criteria for evaluation merit immediate consideration: 1) asking journalists to choose the single organization whose reporting on Latin America they most admire; and 2) asking journalists to choose the single organization they consider the most desirable as a place to work. When asked which organization's reporting on Latin America is most admired, a majority of journalists, about six out of ten, choose either *The New York Times* (34 percent) or the Associated Press (26 percent). When asked to choose the organization they consider the most desirable as a place to work, a majority almost as large (56 percent) choose either *The New York Times* (43 percent) or the Associated Press (13 percent). In each case, foreign affairs journalists select as most admirable or desirable two organizations with vast influence on public opinion, on policy-makers, and on other news organizations. Regarding these two criteria at least, foreign affairs correspondents appear to place less importance on organizational autonomy from marketplace considerations than on organizational power and influence. Whatever the degree of personal autonomy they may enjoy in their daily work roles, most journalists appear to admire some connection with organizations of demonstrable authority and clout.

Performance Concerning Latin America

Most journalists display serious concern for the attention received by Latin America in the U.S. press and for the quality of reporting that region receives. When asked whether their supervisors provided Latin American news with an "appropriate" amount of attention, 40 percent of the respondents said their supervisors gave Latin America less attention than it deserved, and another 20 percent said their supervisors gave Latin America *far* less attention than it deserved. Six out of ten (60 percent) therefore believe their supervisors accord Latin American news less attention than it deserves (see Table 9).

TABLE 9

	Evaluation of Supervisors' Emphasis on News From Latin America	
	%	Cumulative %
More than Deserved	3	3
About Right	37	40
Less than Deserved	40	80
Far Less than Deserved	20	100
	(100)	

Foreign affairs journalists nevertheless believe that U.S. reporting on the region has improved somewhat over the past several years. When asked to evaluate their own organization's reporting on critical events in Latin America, most correspondents believe that reporting on the region has improved in recent years. Only about one out of eight (12 percent) believe that their news organizations' reporting on the Guatemala crisis of 1954 could be considered good (an elected, left-leaning government was overthrown in Guatemala in 1954 by a military coup). And only 24 percent believe that reporting on Castro's ascension to power in Cuba in 1959 can be considered good.

Nevertheless, regarding the Dominican Republic crisis of 1965, during which President Lyndon Johnson sent Marines to that island and interfered with domestic elements there, and during the election of President Salvador Allende Gossens in Chile in 1970, during which a Socialist government was elected in Chile, almost half of the journalists believe that their organizations reported on events in a way that can be considered commendable. Regarding the Dominican Republic crisis, 49 percent believe their organizations reported on that critical event with superior coverage. Regarding the election in Chile in 1970, about 47 percent of the journalists consider their own organizations (the organizations for which they worked at the time) to have provided superior coverage. However much they wish their superiors might pay greater attention to news from Latin America, a growing number of journalists believes that as time passes, the quality of reporting from Latin America is improving. In this respect, journalists' opinions suggest a belief that some kind of gradual learning has occurred, a growing appreciation for accurate reporting on critical events in the Southern Hemisphere.

Informal Personal Networks

Whatever their organizational experience, journalists inhabit an environment permeated with friendships and personal networks. How much interaction do journalists have with other journalists in off-duty relations or with Latin American nationals? How much experience have journalists gathered in some areas of the world which have been theaters of substantial amount of East-West conflict?

Interactions with Other Journalists

This survey reveals clearly that journalists reporting on Latin America for major U.S. publications demonstrate a strong identity with other journalists and with journalism as a profession. They have many friendships among journalists, and in their reporting on Latin America, they are more interested in the challenges it offers to them as professionals, as reporters, than in the intrinsic historical or regional interest of the area.

Strong Identity with Journalism

Respondents in this study appear dedicated to journalism as a career. About 75 percent have fifteen or more years experience as journalists, and 52 percent have twenty-one or more years as journalists. When asked what kind of employment they would like in the next five years, most journalists (67 percent) made it clear that they would prefer to work for the same organization. Another two out of ten (19 percent) would like to work elsewhere in the media. Only 14 percent expressed a preference for working outside the news media (see Table 10).

Other Journalists Are Friends

Consistent with their positive attitudes toward journalism as an occupation, most journalists, about six out of ten (61 percent) report that many or most of their close friends and off-duty contacts are other journalists.

Consistent with their preference for friendships among other journalists, relatively few correspondents have substantial number of friendships with either business executives or government officials. Regarding business executives, only about two out of ten have a substantial number (thirteen or more) friendships with them, while about four out of ten (38 percent) have only a small number (one to ten) of friendships with such executives. About four out of ten (43 percent) have no friendships at all with business executives. Friendships with government officials exhibit similar patterns. Only about one-quarter of the reporters (24 percent) have a substantial

TABLE 10

	Experience As A Journalist (in years)	
	%	Cumulative %
17 or Less	26	26
18 – 20	19	45
21 – 25	16	61
26 or more	39	100
	(100)	

	Preferred Employment Location After Five Years	
	%	Cumulative %
In the Same Organization	67	67
Elsewhere in Journalism	19	86
Outside of Journalism	14	100
	(86)	

number of friendships with officials, about three out of ten (29 percent) have a small number of such friendships, and almost half have no official friends at all.

Although about 60 percent of the respondents report close friendships with other journalists, only a little over half (53 percent) report that they belong to professional associations in journalism. Of those who do belong to professional associations, about half (51 percent) belong to only one and about three out of ten (28 percent) to only two. When asked to name the most important professional associations they belong to, those who did mention the names of specific organizations referred primarily to honorary societies, such as Sigma Delta Chi, or social clubs, such as the Overseas Press Club. Only four belong to any organization that can be considered "trade unionist" in orientation: the Newspaper Guild. Friendship with other journalists is not associated with a substantial amount of activity in professional organizations (see Table 11).

Preference for Career over Region

Consistent with their strong sense of identity as a distinct occupational group, journalists reporting on Latin America appear to place more faith in their professional colleagues generally rather than in those who share an interest in Latin America or in the history and inherent interest of the region. When asked to rate the performance of colleagues reporting on Latin America compared with that of colleagues posted elsewhere, only about half (49 percent) of the respondents consider their colleagues reporting on Latin America to be somewhat better or much better than average.

When asked which goal motivated them in their work, the regional challenges of working in Latin America, its historical interests, its people, and its possibilities for adventure, or the professional challenges of reporting on Latin America, most journalists, about six out of ten (59 percent), said they liked reporting on Latin America not because of its inherent interest as a region but because of the challenges it offers reporters as professional news gatherers. Most journalists reporting on Latin America, therefore, display a strong sense of identity with journalism as a profession, an identity that is stronger on the whole than their interest in Latin America as a region.

Familiarity with Latin America

Journalists who have worked for major U.S. news organizations in reporting on Latin America display a substantial amount of experience in reporting on the region and report close friendships with Latin nationals. Contrary to what some may think, most journalists seem to speak or read Spanish and Portuguese rather well and are relatively cosmopolitan in that they are

TABLE 11   Friendships and Professional Participation

	Proportion of Off-Duty Contacts With Other Journalists			Percent of Time Spent With Business Executive Friends	
	%	Cumulative %		%	Cumulative %
Most	12	12	13% or More	19	19
Many	49	61	1 – 12%	38	57
A Few	31	92	None	43	100
Almost None or None	8	100			—
	(102)			(100)	

	Percent of Time Spent With Government Official Friends			Number of Professional Memberships		
	%	Cumulative %		%	Adjusted %	Cumulative %
13% or More	24	24	No Response	9	0	
1 – 12%	29	53	None	44	0	
None	47	100	One	24	51	51
	100		Two	13	28	79
			Three or More	10	21	100
				(102)		

familiar with an additional foreign language. In their use of sources, journalists appear evenly divided between official and non-official sources.

Substantial Experience Reporting on the Region
Almost six out of ten respondents (59 percent) have reported on Latin America for ten or more years and can, therefore, be assumed to have a substantial amount of experience in reporting on the region (see Table 12).

Friendship with Latin American Nationals
Almost two-thirds (64 percent) of the respondents say that many or most of their off-duty social contacts and close friendships, while they were in Latin America, were with nationals of their host countries. When asked to describe their best friends when they were in Latin America, most reporters (55 percent) said that their best friends were indeed from the region. A similar percent (53 percent) said the native language of their best friends was Spanish or Portuguese. And consistent with their friendship preferences for other journalists, most respondents (57 percent) say that when in Latin America their best friends are usually also reporters (see Table 13).

Language Ability
Correspondents rate themselves quite highly in reading and speaking an Iberian language. Regarding reading, 55 percent claim close-to-native ability, while another 43 percent (for a total of 98 percent) claim easy familiarity. Regarding speaking, 44 percent claim close-to-native fluency, and another four out of ten claim easy familiarity.

But most reporters claim to be familiar with additional foreign languages, other than Spanish or Portuguese. About three out of ten say they are familiar with at least one additional foreign language, and another three out of ten claim familiarity with at least two or more additional languages. Almost six out of ten, therefore, say they have conversational familiarity with at least one foreign language other than Spanish or Portuguese. Jour-

TABLE 12

	Number of Years Experience Reporting about Latin America	
	%	Cumulative %
7 or less	35	35
8 – 14	34	69
15 or More	31	100
	(100)	

TABLE 13 Friendship Patterns

	Native Language of Best Friends %	Best Friends When Posted in Latin America %
Spanish or Portuguese	53	From Latin America 55
English	47	From the United States 43
	(85)	Outside Hemisphere 2
		(88)

	Occupation of Best Friends When in Latin America %	
Other (Usually Foreign Affairs) Reporter	57	—
Local Residents	43	
	100	

TABLE 14

	Reading Familiarity with Spanish or Portuguese %	Speaking Familiarity with Spanish or Portuguese %
Native Fluency or Close to it	55	44
Easy Facility	43	40
Partial Familiarity	1	15
Less Than Partial Familiarity	1	1
	(95)	(94)

	Number of Non-Iberian Languages With Which a Correspondent has Conversational Familiarity %	Cumulative %
None Additional	41	41
One Additional	31	72
Two or More Additional	28	100
	(100)	

nalists reporting on Latin America appear interested in the major languages of the region, but they also appear interested in languages found in other regions and therefore seem rather cosmopolitan (see Table 14).

Sources

When respondents use sources abroad, they appear about equally divided between using official and non-official sources. Official sources include foreign or local governments; non-official sources include foreign and local press, non-official groups generally, and businessmen. About eight out of ten journalists prefer local sources when posted in Latin America to foreign sources (see Table 15).

Familiarity with Crisis Situations

As may be expected, most journalists report more familiarity with, and greater knowledge of, more recent crises than those which happened in the more remote past. In particular, journalists cite some familiarity with the coup in Brazil in 1964, the crisis in the Dominican Republic in 1965, and the election in Chile in 1976.

Journalists report relatively little experience in theaters of substantial East-West conflict, but at least two-thirds (67 percent) have reported from Central America or the Caribbean (where Guatemala in 1954 and Cuba since 1959 have raised a number of East-West issues), and about a third (33 percent) have reported from Western Europe where East-West issues are frequently discussed.

Conclusion

As a group, most correspondents included in this study appear to share a number of characteristics with other professionals whose careers have come to maturity after World War II. They are well-educated, and they exhibit a remarkable amount of organizational stability in their careers.

TABLE 15

	Preferred Sources When Writing About Latin America	
	%	Cumulative %
Foreign Diplomats and Correspondents	21	21
Local officials	40	61
Local Non-Official Groups (including local media)	39 (77)	100

Foreign correspondents also display characteristics that may or may not be shared with other professionals who have entered careers since World War II. Whether through early family experience as first-born children or as children with few siblings, many correspondents have learned early lessons in self-reliance and about three out of ten have remained single or experienced divorce. In addition, almost half (45 percent) attended college in New England or within the New York-Washington, D.C., corridor. And most respondents appear to work in an organizational environment where a relatively small number of organizations (e.g., *The New York Times* or the Associated Press) are regarded as the most desirable employers.

Finally, journalists appear to identify more strongly with their colleagues, or perhaps their "craft," than with the inherent historical and social importance of their region of assignment, in this case Latin America. Journalists appear to identify more with the role of "generalists" who can transfer easily from one regional context to another than with the role of "expert" who learns a great deal about a specific topic. In a society rewarding specialist skills so highly, foreign correspondents, like their domestic counterparts, remain an example of the almost lost tradition of "amateurs."

Notes

1. For a survey of U.S. correspondents based in Europe in the early 1950s see Theodore Edward Kruglak, *The Foreign Correspondents*. Geneva: Librarie E. Droz, 1955. (Reprinted in 1974 by Greenwood Press; Westport, Connecticut)

2. In mail questionnaires, it is customary to regard anything better than a 20 percent response rate as good; in that context, a response race of 76 percent is considered quite good and constitutes a level of response difficult to achieve even in national surveys employing telephones.

3. For a discussion of a similarly curious, privileged correspondent in England, see Peterson, 1979.

4

Learning to Be an "Examiner"

What is an "Examiner"?

Chapter Two suggests the use of "chronicler" and "examiner" to describe two distinct visions of appropriate roles for journalists. Before asking why some journalists are more likely to become "examiners" than others, it is necessary to understand why this study has selected the terms "chronicler" and "examiner," rather than the more traditional dichotomies used to describe two distinct roles journalists play: "gatekeepers" or "advocates," for example, or "neutrals" and "participants."[1]

Two major reporting orientations are admired by journalists today: one orientation admires "objective," restrained, and technically efficient journalism. The other, some say "opposite" orientation, admires "investigative, analytic, and interpretive reporting." (See Johnstone, *et al.* 1976: 114, 116). In searching for the most appropriate terms to describe these two orientations, two criteria can be suggested: historical utility and analytical accuracy. Consider historical utility first.

The Examiner Tradition: Historical Roots

If we examine the way American journalists have thought about their reporting roles historically, we may be able to anchor our descriptions of those roles in ideas that have mattered a great deal to newsgatherers throughout

U.S. history. For example, one way to achieve historical grounding is to examine the titles publishers and editors have selected for their daily newspapers. Newspaper names can be considered to be an index not only of owner intention, but also of what was believed to sell papers at the time. Names, therefore, may reflect what newspaper owners believed readers wanted newspapers to do. Are there two distinct roles for newspapers apparent in the intentions of the founders? Do they reflect the current debates between a relatively detached, dispassionate reporting orientation and a more involved, "participant" one?

A list of newspapers with Washington correspondents provided by Leo Rosten in his pioneering work *The Washington Correspondents* (N.Y.: Harcourt, Brace, 1937; or Arno Press, 1974) can be viewed as a representative sample of the names of the most important papers in the United States. Each employed correspondents in Washington. Each paper can be coded with a noun expressing the predominant social or political role its name suggests. The resulting codes can be compared by searching for role clusters. Two major clusters can be identified and given titles anchored in journalism history and practice. The two cluster titles can be considered distinct political and social newspaper roles not only envisioned by journalists when newspapers were founded, but also significant today. The two orientations are labeled "chronicler" and "examiner."[2] Table 16 lists the newspaper names and coded roles associated with each.

The chronicler perspective embraces all dailies that, through their titles, signify breadth, reliability, and speed. The examiner perspective, by contrast, encompasses names suggesting both guidance and the presentation of choices. The chronicler perspective is found in terms such as bulletin, caller, courier, dispatch, express, mail, mercury, post, and telegraph — all of which suggest speed. Citizen, journal, observer, patriot, and transcript all suggest reliability, at the very least; and gazette, globe, record, and times all convey an impression of thoroughness, of breadth. Some terms may suggest more than one category, but all appear to belong in the umbrella category of "chronicler," a person or organization that composes a historical account of events in their order of occurrence.

The other cluster is quite different. Guardianship, or guidance, is suggested in such titles as beacon, clarion, constitution, guardian, herald, leader, monitor, phoenix, plain dealer, sentinel, star, and tribune. In similar fashion, the presentation of "choices" is illustrated in terms like inquirer, ledger (debits and credits), mirror (showing an honest reflection against which events can be seen and judged), and sun (which sheds light on, illuminates, or presents events in the light of day). Although some names may arguably belong in more than one category, each falls comfortably within the broad scope of an examiner orientation. Both "chronicler" and "examiner" are, of course, themselves derived from the names of daily papers.

TABLE 16   Newspaper Orientation

Chronicler (Breadth, Reliability, Speed)		Examiner (Guidance, Choice)	
Name	Function	Name	Function
Bulletin	speed	Beacon	guidance
Caller	speed	Bee	choice
Chronicle	all categories	Clarion	guidance
Citizen	reliability	Constitution	guidance
Courier	speed	Examiner	guidance, choice
Dispatch	speed	Guardian	guidance
Express	speed	Herald	guidance
Gazette	breadth	Inquirer	choice
Globe	breadth	Leader	guidance
Journal	reliability	Ledger	choice
Mail	speed	Mirror	choice
Mercury	speed	Monitor	guidance
Observer	reliability	Phoenix	guidance
Patriot	reliability	Plain Dealer	guidance
Post	speed	Sentinel	guidance
Record	breadth	Star	guidance
Telegraph	speed	Sun	guidance, choice
Transcript	reliability	Tribune	guidance

Each of these role clusters can be considered to be historial orientations, or models, for journalists to emulate. The chronicler model emphasizes speed, breadth (appeal to a wide audience and attention to unusual events, regarding news as "exception"), and reliability (accuracy and careful attribution). The examiner model, in contrast, emphasizes guidance (providing contextual analysis and interpretation of complex problems) and the presentation of choices. As employed in this study, that presentation may become apparent in at least two ways: discussing national issues before they become cemented in policy and representing the viewpoints and interests of competing groups, especially the viewpoints of excluded and underprivileged groups.

Usefulness as Analytical Tools

Some of the preceding characteristics are similar to those used by John W. C. Johnstone, *et. al.,* to describe what they refer to as "neutral" and "participant" belief sets. (Johnstone, *et. al.,* 1976:118). Yet what the Johnstone group labels these two orientations, "Neutral" and "participant" roles, styles, functions, or "belief sets," is troublesome. The neutral-participant dichotomy suggests that one role is extremely passive, the other extremely active. Given these choices, an intelligent reader is tempted to assume that almost every reporter might fall into some version of the "participant" category, since the absolute "neutrality" of journalists or even newspapers, public institutions with public functions, is difficult to imagine. Although "neutrality" defined as "impartiality" is enshrined in the conventions and codes of journalism, its usefulness as a descriptive tool is suspect.

The categories of neutral and participant therefore may shrink one category (neutral) and enlarge another (participant) so much that readers and social scientists are deprived of useful analytical constructs. The suggested categories of chronicler and examiner, by contrast, recognize that all reporters and newspapers are in some sense social participants, playing distinguishable social roles. The proposed categories also carry the advantage of roots in newspaper tradition and practice, enjoying perhaps a presumptive historical validity.

As mentioned in an earlier chapter, "chronicler" and "examiner" are also preferable to "gatekeeper" and "advocate." The category "gatekeeper" is so all encompassing that it can include almost every professional journalist. Much narrower is the term "advocate," which connotes a smaller number of journalists representing groups that normally have little access to the media. The term "examiner," compared to the category of "advocate," is far more sweeping and carries a sense of judicious deliberation. In addition, it enjoys a firm historical connection which the "advocacy" perspective lacks, if we are to judge by the names of most newspapers.

This is not to deny that in certain important periods in our history "advocacy" journalism has played an important role. Thomas Paine's *Common Sense* was, of course, an advocate of colonial autonomy. In a less honorable tradition, the role of William Randolph Hearst in abetting the Spanish-American War was also an example of advocacy journalism. But if we are to use categories derived from our most important and oldest newspapers, then the examiner role appears more acceptable to most journalists.

The Examiner Role: Ignored in Codes of Ethics

To recall the valiant origins of the examiner model is not to claim that its expectations are formally acknowledged in contemporary codes of journalistic responsibility. A special Commission on Freedom of the Press (the "Hutchins Commission") issued a book in 1947 called *A Free and Responsible Press: A General Report on Mass Communication: Newspapers, Radio, Motion Pictures, Magazines, and Books* (Chicago: University of Chicago Press, 1947). In it, the Commission made five main recommendations regarding the proper function of journalism. One urged that "the press must provide full access to the day's intelligence," similar to one of the characteristics of the chronicler model, thoroughness. The other four recommendations appear to fall rather cleanly under the requirements of the "examiner" model:

1) the press must give a truthful, comprehensive, and intelligent account of the day's events in a *context* which gives them meaning; 2) the press must provide a forum for the *exchange of comment and criticism;* 3) the press must project a *representative picture of the constituent groups in the society;* and 4) the press must *present and clarify the goals and values* of the society (emphases added). (Commission recommendations reported in J. C. Thomson, 1978:8).

Despite the injunction of this Commission to pay special attention to examiner performance functions, a close review of the major codes of ethics developed by the journalism profession reveals almost no attention at all given to these criteria, recommendations which one observer ennobled collectively with the illustrious title, "a theory of responsibility." (Paraphrased in W. H. Ferry, "Masscomm as Guru," in J. C. Merrill and R. D. Barnery, eds., 1975:48; quoted in J. Thomson, 1978:8).[3] The American Society of Newspaper Editors (ASNE) in 1923 fashioned a "Code of Ethics or Canons of Journalism" and issued in 1975 "A Statement of Principles," updating the older code, while Sigma Delta Chi, the Society of Professional Journalists, composed a "Code of Ethics" in 1973. (See Appendices I, II, III in J. Thomson, 1978:14–16). A careful reading of these codes demonstrates an almost exclusive focus on chronicler newspaper criteria and functions. The 1973 Sigma Delta Chi code in Article IV, Section 7, even seems to specify the importance not of "representative constituent groups," but of expertise in recommending that:

Journalists recognize their responsibility for offering *informed* analysis, comment, and editorial opinion on public events and issues. They accept the obligation to present such material by individuals whose *competence, experience,* and *judgment* qualify them for it (Code of Ethics, Article IV, Section 7).

The 1923 ASNE Code of Ethics contains seven articles, while the 1973 Code and the 1975 ASNE Statement of Princples each list six. Yet only the second paragraph of Article I, titled "responsibility" in the 1975 Statement, makes any prescription that even remotely resembles examiner news functions, namely: "The American press was made free not just to inform or just to serve as a forum for debate, but also to bring an independent scrutiny to bear on the forces of power in the society, including the conduct of official power at·all levels of government." (quoted in Thomson, 1978:15). In recent history, professional conceptions of appropriate performance criteria for newspapers seem to have changed little. Modern professional thinking pays scant attention to altruistic admonishments to function more as examiners, failing to exalt the aspirations of the Commission on Freedom of the Press.

Despite the absence of attention to "examining" displayed in codes and statements, the examiner perspective is nevertheless important. Historically, it expresses the combined thrust of newspaper names and the intentions of newspaper founders. Responsibly, it represents serious efforts to reform journalism, exemplified in the 1947 Hutchins Commission report.

Measuring An "Examiner" Perspective

In order to understand how the complex concept of "examining" can be packaged into a single measure or dimension, it is useful to outline the procedure used to construct an examiner "scale." Table IV-2 reveals the individual attitude items tested in order to devise a one-dimensional scale. It is noteworthy that most foreign affairs respondents consider "examining" essential or very important. They are much more ambivalent about "chronicler" orientation (see Table 17).

As defined, examiner and chronicler orientations are usually considered to be "opposing" viewpoints. Emphasizing the careful analysis, examination, and investigation of opinions is assumed to require too much time or to receive less than highest priority for those who believe absolutely that information must always be transmitted rapidly, that one should concentrate on news of interest to the widest possible public, and that one should stay away from stories where factual content cannot be (easily) verified. These two perspectives are assumed at variance with one another. Someone who examines a great deal is unlikely to value highly what chroniclers value.

In order to test the validity of this assumption, and in order to construct a single composite index measuring support for an examining orientation, all items listed in Table 17 were clustered using a variety of mathematical procedures (factor analysis and Guttman scaling) to determine which attitude items best satisfy two criteria: they must be strongly related to one another (that is, they all must measure the *same underlying attitude* or broad orientation); and they must be arranged in some *range* or in an *ascending hierarchy* from widespread agreement to less widespread agreement. Those who agree with the items for which it is more difficult to find widespread agreement must be found, statistically, to also agree with the attitudes for which there is widespread agreement. The two requirements for this kind of scale, called a Guttman scale, are therefore that all attitude items on the scale measure the same underlying dimension and that they be arranged in some kind of hierarchy or rank order across a range of opinions, from those easiest to agree with to those most difficult to agree with.

Using those criteria, a composite scale can be constructed, using the four items arranged as described in Table 18. Since these four items form a single scale, our analysis reveals that examiner and chronicler orientations are, as expected, opposing perspectives. Someone who considers "essential" the investigation of claims and statements made by the government is likely to consider less than essential several journalistic conventions favored by chroniclers: getting information to the public as quickly as possible, concentrating on news which is of interest to the widest possible public, and staying away from stories where factual content cannot be verified. The summary table at the bottom of Table 18 shows the overall distribution of attitudes for

TABLE 17 How important do you consider each of the following statements as codes or conventions guiding the practice of journalism?

	Essential %	Very Important %	Important %	Seldom Important %	Not Important At All %	Total Percent %	Total Number
1. Examiner Statements (The more essential, the more "examining" the orientation)							
*a. Discuss national policy while it is still being developed	74	16	8	1	1	100	(101)
*b. Provide analysis and interpretation of complex problems	64	28	8	0	0	100	(102)
*c. Investigate claims and statements made by the government	55	35	8	2	0	100	(101)
d. Prepresent the viewpoints and interests of competing groups, especially those of excluded and under-privileged groups	44	19	18	8	11	100	(94)
2. Chronicler Statements (The more essential, the more like a chronicler the orientation)							
*a. Get information to the public as quickly as possible	38	25	30	5	2	100	(102)
*b. Concentrate on news of interest to the widest possible public	32	18	42	7	1	100	(101)
*c. Stay away from stories where factual content cannot be verified	22	15	26	20	17	100	(96)

*Asterisked items are drawn from John W. C. Johnstone, et. al., 1976: 230.

73

the composite examiner scale. About six out of ten (59 percent) respondents are most favorable or very favorable toward the examiner perspective (see Table 18).

Historical and Lifecycle Factors

In examining historical and life cycle factors related to an examining perspective, it becomes clear that the reporters most likely to be examiners are young achievers with few siblings. Seven out of ten (72 percent) of those 40 or younger are strong examiners, compared to about five out of ten respondents forty-one years-of-age or more who are strong examiners. Respondents with fewer than three siblings are more likely to be examining than those with three or more. About seven out of ten respondents who have fewer than three siblings are examiners, compared to only five out of ten who have three or more. Young reporters who acquired early experience in self-reliance are relatively examining.

Examiners tend to major in the humanities and journalism and to earn advanced degrees. About eight out of ten (78 percent) humanities majors and six out of ten journalism majors are examiners, compared to only about 45 percent of social-science majors. In addition, having earned a Masters

TABLE 18

	Examiner Scale
Essential 55%	Investigate claims and statements made by the government
Less Than Essential 62%	Get information to the public as quickly as possible
Less Than Essential 68%	Concentrate on news which is of interest to the widest possible public
Less Than Essential 78%	Stay away from stories where factual content cannot be verified

Coefficient of Reproducibility = .78

	Examiner Orientation (Overall Distribution) %
Most Favorable	21
Very Favorable	38
Somewhat Favorable	26
Least Favorable	15
	(95)

( ) = absolute number

degree is somewhat related to an examining orientation. Seventy-three percent of those with an M.A. are strong examiners, compared to only 62 percent of those with bachelor's degree. Youth, early self-reliance, a humanist
orientation, and educational achievement are both linked to the acquisition
of an examining perspective (see Table 19).

Organizational Factors

The organizational factors associated with an examining perspective are consistent with the historical and personal characteristics of high examiners.
Those who have achieved a great deal, given their youth, and those who
value autonomy in their work roles are likely to favor an examining perspective strongly.

Individual Status Characteristics: Income and Editorial Experience

Those with incomes between the highest and lowest are most likely to be examining. About seven out of ten of those whose annual incomes lie between
$27,500 and $37,500 are strong examiners, compared to only somewhat
more than five out of ten of those with lower or higher incomes. Young people who have not the lowest, but rather middle-range incomes, are reporters
who have achieved a great deal for their age.

Regarding editing experience, those who currently already spend at least
a moderate proportion of their time editing, as opposed to reporting, are
somewhat more likely to be examining. About seven out of ten (67 percent)
of those who spend a moderate amount of time editing (over 5 percent of
their time) are likely to be very examining, compared to less than six out of
ten (56 percent) of those who spend no time at all editing and less than five
out of ten (44 percent) who spend more than 40 percent of their time editing.

Consistent with their position as young achievers, strong examiners are
somewhat likely to believe that their supervisors exert considerable control
over their outputs and assignments. Of those who are the most highly examining, about seven out of ten (69 percent) believe they have very little
authority or control over their output and assignments, compared to about
six out of ten (57 percent) who believe they have considerable control over
their assignments. At the same time, among the most examining respondents, about two-thirds (36 percent) say they operate primarily as individuals, compared to only 15 percent who say they operate as team members at
least 50 percent of the time (see Table 20).

TABLE 19 Examiner Orientation by Age, Number of Siblings, College Major, and Highest Degree

	Age			Number of Siblings		
	40 or less %	41–50 %	51 or more %	0 or 1 %	(2) %	3 or more %
High	19	11	31	High or Medium 65	68	50
Examining Medium	53	45	22	Low 35	32	50
Low	28	56	47	(43)	(22)	(30)
	(36)	(27)	(32)			

prob = .06*   prob = .07

	College Major			Highest Degree	
	Social Sciences %	Humanities %	Journalism %	B.A. %	M.A. %
High or Medium	45	78	60	High or Medium 62	73
Examining Low	55	22	40	Low 38	27
	(22)	(32)	(25)	(60)	(22)

prob = .18   prob = .07

*The lower the probability, the stronger the relationship between two factors.

76

TABLE 20 Examiner Orientation by Income, Editing Experience, and Team Experience

	Highest Annual Income				Current Editing Responsibilities (In Percent of Time)		
	Less than $27,500 %	$27,500 – $37,500 %	More than $37,500 %		None %	Less than 5% %	40% or more %
Examining High or Medium	55	71	56	High or Medium	67	56	44
Low	45 (33)	29 (35)	44 (27)	Low	33 (52)	44 (23)	56 (16)
prob = .60				prob = .23			

	Teamwork Context	
	Individual %	Team (At least 50% of time) %
Examining High	35.5	15
Medium	29	46
Low	35.5 (31)	39 (61)
prob = .06		

News Organization Characteristics

Select Audience Market

Not only are those who believe they have relatively little authority over their output and assignments relatively high examiners, but those who work in organizations with high-select markets are also likely to be highly examining as well. Three out of ten (31 percent) of those who work in organizations that target their news at select audiences (the major daily newspapers and newsweeklies) register a very strong examining orientation,, compared to only about one out of ten (9 percent) of those who work for organizations devoted primarily to broad national markets, such as the Associated Press (AP) and United Press International (UPI) (see Table 21).

Performance Evaluation

Consistent with their youth, their high achievements, and their concern for work-role autonomy, those who maintain a critical distance from the reporting of their own organizations are likely to be highly examining. In general, those who do not rank at all, or those who rank as only poor or fair their own organization's reporting on the Dominican Republic crisis in 1965 or the Chilean crisis in 1970, are likely to be more examining than those who rank their own organization's performance as good, very good, or outstanding during those crises.

Over nine out of ten (94 percent) who are familiar with their own organization's reporting on the Dominican crisis of 1965 and who found it lacking are strong examiners, compared to only four out of ten (44 percent) of those who ranked their own organizations' performance highly in that crisis. In a similar fashion, about eight out of ten (80 percent) of those who are familiar with reporting on the election of President Salvador Allende of Chile and found it lacking are highly examining. Yet only five out of ten (50 percent) of those who ranked their own organizations highly during the coverage of the Chilean election are similarly examining.

Personal Network Factors

Consistent with the finding that young achievers are likely to be highly examining, reporters with relatively few years reporting in general, and few years reporting on Latin America specifically, are likely to be highly examining. In parallel fashion, those who have failed to form many friendships with Latin Americans or with many correspondents abroad are likely to be examining. For all their lack of experience covering Latin America, however,

TABLE 21 Examiner Orientation by Organization Respondent Worked for Longest

	Broad Market (Wire Services) %	Select Market (Other) %
High	9	31
Examining		
Medium	49	33
Low	42	36
	(43)	(52)

prob = .03

	Wire Service %	Major Newspapers %	Major Weeklies %	N.Y. Times Washington Post %
High or Medium	58	69	80	48
Examining				
Low	42	31	20	52
	(43)	(16)	(15)	(21)

prob = .02

young examiners are nevertheless relatively cosmopolitan, both in their selection of friendships from outside of journalism and in their tendency to know more than one foreign language.

Few Years of Experience

Because of their youth, the achievement-oriented examiners tend to have few years of experience in reporting on Latin America. Those with fourteen or fewer years general reporting experience are most likely to be examining. Concerning experience in reporting on Latin America, specifically, those with seven or fewer years experience in reporting on the region are similarly most likely to be examining. It should be pointed out in addition that the second-largest proportion of examiners is found in the middle categories of experience: fifteen to twenty-five years of reporting generally, and eight to fourteen years of reporting on Latin America specifically (see Table 22).

Little Familiarity with Latin America

It might be expected that those who are most integrated into friendships with Latin Americans are the most likely to be examining. Because of their concern for and interest in their Latin friends, those with many friendships among host country nationals might be expected to act more critically, to be more concerned with investigative, analytical reports, and to examine government statements, whether released by the local authorities or the U.S. government, with considerable care. This expectation is not confirmed.

Consistent with their youth and lack of experience, most examiners have relatively little familiarity with Latin Americans. About seven out of ten (71 percent) of those who say they have few Latin friends are very examining, whereas only 56 percent of those with many Latin friends are examiners. Similarly, about seven out of ten (72 percent) of those whose primary friends abroad are English-speaking are examiners, whereas only about five out of ten (54 percent) of those with primarily Spanish- or Portuguese-speaking friends are examiners. In parallel fashion, about seven out of ten (72 percent) of those whose best friends are from the United States are likely to be examining, but only a little over five out of ten (56 percent) of those whose best friends are from Latin America are likely to manifest examining tendencies.

The finding that examiners have fewer friendships with Latin Americans than non-examiners can be attributed more to youth and reporting inexperience than to lack of curiosity and interest. It is clear, for example, that the self-reported reading and speaking ability of Spanish and Portuguese examiners is equal to the self-ratings of non-examiners. This equivalence may result from the circumstance that most correspondents who report from Latin America are relatively well trained in Spanish and Portuguese prior to arrival. But the interest of these young examiners extends beyond Latin

TABLE 22 Examiner Orientation by Experience as a Journalist and as a Reporter Covering Latin America

	Years as a Journalist		
	14 or Less	15—25	26 or More
	%	%	%
High	28	15	22
Examining Medium	44	56	22
Low	28	29	56
	(25)	(34)	(36)

prob = .03

	Years Reporting on Latin America		
	7 or less	8—14	15 or More
	%	%	%
High	30	12	19
Medium	30	56	35
Low	40	32	46
	(33)	(34)	(26)

prob = .16

America. About eight out of ten (79 percent) who speak one additional foreign language other than an Iberian one tend to be examining compared to only five out of ten (54 percent) of those who know only Spanish or Portuguese (see Table 23).

Curiosity about the Region

The curiosity of these young examiners about Latin America as a region and about a world beyond journalism is easily apparent. Those who like their work less because of the challenges it offers respondents as reporters than because the Latin American region has intrinsic historical, political, and other interests are relatively examining. Twenty-eight percent who believe the region has inherent interest are examiners, compared to only 15 percent who like their jobs because they offer challenges to news-reporting skills. Young examiners extend their friendships beyond journalists to people from many different occupations. Those who have many journalist friends in general are about equally likely as those with many non-journalist friends to be examiners. But in focusing on friendships abroad in the field, about seven out of ten (74 percent) of those whose host-country friends are local professional and neighborhood contacts tend to be examiners, compared to only 55 percent of those whose best friends are primarily other correspondents. Although inexperienced, young examiners are curious about the region they report from and about friendships beyond the world of journalism. Their friendship networks, given their youth, may be relatively fluid and expanding.

Little Direct Experience with East-West Issues

Because of their youth and because they have experienced little interaction with military and diplomatic sources, those with the least amount of personal experience in reporting on arenas or theaters of East-West conflict are likely to be rather examining. For example, within Latin America, two-

TABLE 23   Examiner Orientation by Regional Origin of Best Friends

	Best Friends When in Latin America	
	From the United States %	From Latin America %
High or medium Examining	72	56
Low	28	44
	(38)	(45)
prob = .15		

thirds (67 percent) of those who say they were *not* familiar professionally with the 1959 ascension of power of Fidel Castro in Cuba are examiners, compared to only about four out of ten (37 percent) of those who report knowing that episode well.

Those who have reported from theatres of East-West conflict outside the hemisphere are also quite likely to be less examining than those who have not reported from those locations. About two-thirds (65 percent) of those who have not reported from East Asia or China are examiners, whereas only 50 percent of those who have reported from there are examiners. A similar two-thirds (67 percent) of those who have not reported from Western Europe are likewise examiners, compared to only 50 percent who do have such reporting experience.

These findings suggest that those who have experience in reporting on some conflict locations are likely to be less examining than those who are innocent of such experiences. One possible reason for this discovery is that those without reporting experience in areas of high conflict have interacted less with military, diplomatic, and other strategic thinkers, and therefore, may have formed fewer social contacts and friendships with such sources. As a result, novice reporters may display fewer shared beliefs and values.

Conclusion

Two perspectives on professional reporting, one called "chronicler," the other "examiner," are rooted in journalistic history and useful in describing reporters today. This study of foreign affairs reporters suggests that examiners tend to be young and given a scarcity of siblings, accustomed to responsibility at an early age. Examiners also tend to be humanities or journalism majors with advanced degrees.

Young achievers in terms of income and editing experience, they are often free from the constraints of working for the hourly deadlines associated with a major wire-service organization targeted toward broad markets. Believing somewhat that they lack autonomy in making news decisions, examiners are somewhat critical of modern crisis coverage (involving expressed East-West issues), for example the Dominican Republic episode in 1965 and the election of President Salvador Allende in Chile in 1970.

Examiners tend to be less experienced in journalism or reporting on Latin America than non-examiners, and as a result have fewer Latin American friends than North American friends. At the same time, however, they appear cosmopolitan and interested not simply in journalism as a profession, but also in Latin America as a region. If their friendship networks follow their curiosity in the future, they may grow to include many more Latin nationals than they do presently.

Examiners tend *not* to have gathered professional reporting experience in some major arenas of East-West conflicts: Cuba (1959), Western Europe, and the Far East or China. This lack of experience may simply be related to youth, but it may also suggest that examiners have interacted relatively llittle with other experts — military, diplomtic, and otherwise — during an immediate crisis of strategic moment. Such field experiences may have considerable power in forming attitudes in the crucible of a crisis. Examiners typically lack such experiences and, presumably, some of the friendship networks that those experiences generate.

Notes

1. Recognizing the imprecision in these contrasting visions, scholars have attempted to flesh out their characteristics by referring to different empirical domains. Describing the variety of roles played by foreign affairs reporters interacting with officials in Washington, D.C., Bernard Cohen outlined three neutral roles (informer to the public, interpreter of news, and instrument of government — in that official policies and statements are faithfully reported), and four participant (policy) roles (representative of the public, critic of government, advocate of policy, and policy-maker). Cohen composed his list of roles after interviewing many foreign affair journalists (1963). Robert Batscha enumerated three additional roles (in addition to the neutral and participant orientations) he discovered among broadcast journalists, terming them: visualizer of events, catalyst for newspapers, and instant and continuous national chronicler of transpiring events (Batscha, 1975:26). Both Cohen and Batscha derive their role orientations from relatively recent empirical observation of news gathers.

2. Names only are coded; whether each paper functioned in any way consistent with its name is a question too complex to be answered here.

3. Mr. Thomson is the Curator of the Nieman Foundation, Harvard University.

5

Colleagues or Adversaries

Cooperation and Conflict

Although the watchdog function of the press is hallowed in belief and practice in domestic affairs, for a number of journalists, as for other professionals, challenging officials stops at the water's edge. A serious dilemma confronts professional journalists when reporting on crises abroad. How much should officials be relied on for advice, and how much can they be challenged before reporters lose their support entirely as essential pipelines of government information? In order to explore the ways reporters covering Latin America for major U.S. news institutions resolve that dilemma, reporters were asked about their perspectives in two situations: when confronting officials in the field, in Latin America itself; and when encountering officials in Washington, D.C. It is obviously important to know how journalists regard officials in the field, where immediate crises are often found. It is also important to learn how journalists regard officials in Washington, where so many policies affecting the resolution of crises are shaped.

Respondents were asked two simple questions to explore their perspectives on patterns of behavior between reporters and officials. They were asked if they would describe relations between reporters and U.S. officials stationed in Latin America as always collegial, usually collegial, somewhat collegial, somewhat adversarial, usually adversarial, or always adversarial. They were also asked which of the preceding categories they would use to describe relations between reporters and U.S. officials in Washington, D.C. Regarding journalist-official interaction in latin America, about two-thirds of the respondents (67 percent) said they considered relations between reporters and officials as collegial (somewhat, usually, or always). The other third regarded such relations as adversarial. In contrast with their views on such relations in Latin America, however, a minority of about four out of ten (42 percent) of the respondents regard relations between reporters and officials as collegial in Washington, D.C., while a majority, about six out of ten (58 percent), regard such relations in the nation's capital as adversarial. A possible explanation for this discrepancy is that when journalists report on crises abroad, editors at home often wish to know the official U.S. position on that crisis. Learning about official policy abroad may require very good relations between reporters and officials stationed there, and may account at least partially for the high level of reporter cooperation between reporters and officials in the field (see Table 24).

Reporters and Officials in Latin America

Although only a third of the respondents are likely to challenge officials abroad substantially, it is useful to explore the factors that make journalists more adversarial than others when posted abroad.

Lifecycle Factors

Regarding the early experiences of reporters likely to challenge officials, one of the clearest findings is that those who have completed bachelor's degrees in the social sciences, as opposed to those majoring in the humanities or in journalism, are quite likely to challenge officials abroad. Completing a major in the social sciences represents a fascination with people in groups, an interest not simply in individuals but in broad patterns of human interaction and behavior. This suggests an interest in broad political, historical, and social trends, as opposed to a more focused interest in vignettes and stories. Reporters who are adversarial abroad may also tend, though to a lesser extent, to have had some military experience, to have an M.A., and to be under forty-one or over fifty years of age. These factors all may have some bearing on a reporter's learning to challenge officials, but the most significant lifecycle factor affecting that orientation is a broad perspective developed relatively early in a reporter's career, manifested in a decision to major in one of the social sciences. About seven out of ten (68 percent) of the social-science majors are adversarial compared with only about three out of ten (27

TABLE 24 Adversarial Orientations

	Field Adversary				Capital (D.C.) Adversary			
	%	Cumulative %	Adjusted	%	%	Cumulative %	Adjusted	%
Adversarial								
Always	1	1			1	1		
Usually	7	8			13	14		
Somewhat	25	33	High	33	44	58	High	58
Collegial								
Somewhat	30	63	Medium	30	27	85		
Usually	35	98			14	99	Low	42
Always	2	100	Low	37	1	100		
	(95)			(95)	(71)			(71)

		Field Adversary		
		Low	Medium	High
		%	%	%
Capital	High	27	71	71
Adversary	Low	73	29	29
		(22)	(24)	(21)

prob = .003

87

percent) of humanities and two out of ten (22 percent) of journalism majors (see Table 25).

Organizational Factors

Those who challenge officials in the field tend to exhibit three major organizational characteristics: they are employed by some news organizations focusing on highly selective markets; they have gathered a considerable amount of managerial and editorial experience; and they make discriminating judgments in evaluating coverage of crises in Latin America.

Those who challenge officials abroad tend to have worked for long periods of time for particular news institutions that target their product at highly selected markets. Almost half (47 percent) of those who have worked a long time for the *Washington Post* or *The New York Times* are likely to challenge officials abroad along with 44 percent of those who work for one of the prestigious news weeklies. Only three out of ten (30 percent) of wire-service reporters, however, and about one out of ten (12 percent) of those with daily papers other than the two mentioned are likely to be challengers.

In addition to having worked a long time at specific news organizations, most challengers have acquired a considerable amount of managerial and editing experience, especially in Latin America itself. Forty-four percent with some editing experience in Latin America are adversarial, compared with only about three out of ten (29 percent) who have had no editing experience there at all. In a similar fashion, those who are currently engaged in a considerable amount of managerial and editing activities, who supervise a sizable number of employees, and who have a substantial amount of power over their hiring and firing are also likely to challenge officials in the field (see Table 26).

At the same time, journalists who display adversarial perspectives are likely to make well-considered judgments about journalism generally and crisis reporting in particular. A large portion of them appear to accept the amount of attention given Latin America by their superiors. Almost four out of ten of those who believe their supervisors have given Latin American news about the right or slightly less than the amount of coverage it deserves are adversarial, compared with only 15 percent of those who believe the region receives far too little attention. The challengers have also formed clear concepts about excellence in foreign affairs reporting. Almost half (47 percent) of those who judge the quality of crisis reporting by the amount of interpretation and analysis it proves are adversarial, compared with only about three out of ten (31 percent) who judge crisis reporting by speed, accuracy, and breadth.

Holding relatively clear views about quality in crisis reporting, adver-

TABLE 25 Field Opposition, by College Major, Educational Level, Military Experience and Age

	College Major				Educational Level	
	Social Sciences %	Humanities %	Journalism %		B.A. %	M.A. %
Field Adversary High	68	27	22	High or Medium	60	76
Medium or Low	32	73	78	Low	40	24
	(19)	(33)	(27)		(60)	(21)
	prob = .01				prob = .40	

	Military Experience			Age		
	No %	Yes %		40 or Under %	41–50 %	51 or Over %
Field Adversary High	38	26	High or Medium	66	52	70
Medium or Low	62	74	Low	34	48	30
	(52)	(43)		(35)	(27)	(33)
	prob = .18			prob = .65		

TABLE 26 Field Opposition, by Employing News Organization, Field Editing Experience, and Supervisory Authority

	Employing Organization			
	Broad Market (Wire Service)	(Major Dailies)	Select Market (Major Weeklies)	(N.Y. Times Wash. Post)
	%	%	%	%
Field Adversary High	30	12	44	47
Medium or Low	70	8	56	53
	(43)	(17)	(16)	(19)

prob = .23

	Field Editing Experience		Number of Employees Supervised	
	None	Some	5 or Fewer	6 or More
	%	%	%	%
Field Adversary High	29	44	28	46
Medium or Low	71	56	72	54
	(69)	(23)	(71)	(21)

prob = .02   prob = .20

sarial reporters are likely to hold their colleagues' reporting on the region to standards of strict accountability. Among those who believe their colleagues' reporting on Latin America for major U.S. publications are only *average* or *below average* as professional reporters, in comparison with journalists reporting on foreign affairs elsewhere, about four out of ten (37 percent) are adverarial. Only about three out of ten (28 percent) who believe their own colleagues reporting on the region is *better* than average are also likely to be adversarial toward officials.

In harmony with their discriminating judgments about professional reporting and their own colleagues, challengers are likely to display firm convictions about two major critical events in crisis reporting: the ascension to power of Fidel Castro in 1959 in Cuba and the election of President Salvador Allende in Chile in 1970. Over half (56 percent) of those who believe that coverage of Cuba was only poor or fair in the news organizations they worked for at the time are adversarial towards officials, compared with only 8 percent of those who thought reporting on that crisis was quite accomplished. Challengers to officials generally regard coverage of Cuba in 1959 critically.

In contrast, however, they believe improvement in crisis coverage has occurred between 1959 and 1970, when Salvador Allende was elected in Chile. About four out of ten (40 percent) who consider coverage of that election an example of good professional reporting are adversarial, compared to only one out of four (25 percent) who thought it only fair or who did not participate in reporting on that crisis as professional reporters. Reporters who challenge officials in the field are likely to make well-informed, finely discriminating judgments about the quality of crisis coverage in their own organizations. They also appear to believe that coverage may have improved and that some lessons about crisis coverage may have been learned during the 1960s (see Table 27).

Network Factors

The critical perspective shared by those who challenge officials in Latin America suggests that journalists with adversarial orientations are likely to be the types of professionals who largely chart their own occupational courses. After examining the social networks in which challengers are embedded, three observations are clear: they operate independently, maintaining few friendships with other journalists; they have a genuine interest in excellent reporting in their region of assignment; and they tend to have prior or present reporting experience in East-West trouble spots.

Consistent with their critical distance from colleagues reporting on the region, challengers tend to have few journalist friends. About four out of ten

TABLE 27 Field Opposition, by Evaluations of Supervisor Attitude Toward Latin News and of Own News Organization's Coverage of Cuba and Chile

| | | Estimated Supervisor Attention to Latin America | | |
		Far too Little %	Slightly Less Than Deserved %	About Right %
Field Adversary	High	15	36	38
	Medium or Low	85	64	62
		(20)	(36)	(39)

prob = .17

| | | Own Organization's Coverage of Cuba 1959 | | Own Organization's Coverage of Chile 1970 | |
		Poor or Fair %	Excellent or Good %	Poor or Fair %	Excellent or Good %
Field Adversary	High	56	8	25	40
	Medium or Low	44	92	75	60
		(16)	(24)	(16)	(43)

prob = .13

(42 percent) of the respondents who have few friends or no friends at all who are journalists are challengers, compared with one out of four (26 percent) who report that many or most of their friends are journalists. In a similar fashion, this study reveals that adversarial perspectives are found most often among those who belong to at most one professional organization or no professional organization at all.

Although they maintain a critical distance from colleagues, most challengers appear to display a genuine interest in reporting on Latin America in a highly professional manner. Those who travel most outside capital cities in Latin America are consistently the most adversarial journalists, in particular those who travel three months or more in smaller town or cities. Challengers also tend to exhibit an interest in at least one language other than Spanish or Portuguese.

This does not suggest, however, that they are overwhelmingly cosmopolitan. They appear to learn or want to learn thoroughly the languages useful in their work. Those who are not likely to challenge officials tend to speak and read only one foreign language on the one hand, or many foreign languages on the other. Challengers are likely to learn those languages that are necessary to maintain professional reporting standards. In general, challengers have somewhat more years experience reporting on Latin America than do those less likely to challenge officials. Consistent with their other professional attributes, challengers are also more likely than non-challengers to establish contacts with non-official groups, such as newspaper editors, reporters, private sector leaders, and labor leaders in the country of assignment (see Table 28).

Interested in travel outside the capital city and languages useful for the exercise of the profession, preferring unofficial to official contacts in their country of assignment, and displaying many years of experience in reporting on Latin America, those likely to challenge government officials regard their profession as a serious calling. This does not suggest that challengers are likely to establish close friendships with nationals of the countries to which they are assigned. Challengers appear no more nor less likely than non-challengers to regard Latin Americans as close friends. What they do display, nevertheless, is a consistent seriousness in learning a great deal about their countries of assignment all in the service of superior performance as working journalists.

Finally, consistent with their dedication to professional journalism, challengers are likely to have gathered prior reporting experience in East-West trouble spots, particularly in Western Europe, Central America, but also to some extent in both North and Sub-Saharan Africa. Reporting on Chile may have served as a critical event for journalists likely to challenge officials. About half (50 percent) who report considerable amount of familiarity with reporting on the election of Salvador Allende in Chile in 1970 are

TABLE 28   Field Opposition, by Friendships with Other Journalists, Experience Outside Capital Cities, Language Proficiency, and Regional Reporting Experience

	Friendships with Other Journalists		Travel Outside Capital Cities	
	No or Few Friends %	Many or Most %	Less than 3 Months %	3 Months or More %
Field Adversary				
High	42	26	14	39
Medium or Low	56	74	86	61
	(38)	(57)	(22)	(66)
	prob = .11		prob = .08	

	Language Familiarity Beyond Iberian Languages			Years Reporting on Latin America		
	One %	Two %	Three or More %	7 or less %	8-14 %	15 or More %
Field Adversary						
High	31	43	21	26	30	43
Medium or Low	69	57	69	74	70	57
	(35)	(30)	(28)	(34)	(33)	(28)
	prob = .23			prob = .71		

adversarial, while only about three out of ten who know that crisis only somewhat well or not at all are similarly adversarial.

Considered in brief, journalists likely to challenge officials in the field tend to have majored in social-science disciplines and to be interested in studying people in groups. They are likely to work for news organizations appealing to selected news markets, to have amassed considerable managerial and editorial experience, and to make discriminating judgments about the quality of reporting. They are furthermore likely to maintain few friendships with other journalists and to be dedicated to learning a great deal about their regions of assignment. They are also experienced reporters with significant experience abroad, sometimes in East-West trouble spots, and display several years of experience in reporting on Latin America.

Reporters and Officials in Washington, D.C.

Journalists who are adversarial in the field display somewhat different orientations from those journalists who are adversarial in the nation's capital.

Lifecycle Factors

Early family experiences appear more important in their impact on those likely to be adversarial toward colleagues in Washington than they do on adversaries likely to challenge officials in the field. Early experiences and responsibility are quite important. Sixty-five percent of the respondents who are first-born children in their families are relatively adversarial, compared with only 51 percent of those born later. Family size also appears to have an impact on adult capacity to challenge officials in the capital city. Respondents from small families in which there were only one or two children, or alternatively from large families in which there were four or more children, are far more likely to be adversarial than are those from families where there were only three children. About six out of ten (61 percent) respondents from families with only one or two children and seven out of ten respondents from families with four or more children are quite adversarial, compared to only four out of ten respondents from families where there were three children.

It is plausible to suggest in each of the preceding circumstances, where respondents are first-born or from very small or large families, that the burden thrust on each child is considerable. There is a literature on socialization in families that suggests that first-born children and children from families where there are ony one or two children are invested with a considerable sense of responsibility from an early age, since the parents rely so much on such children to carry on the biological family and the wishes of the parents. In the case of large families, each child must learn to challenge in order to carve out a personal identity for himself. In each of the preceding situations, it is plausible that respondents have experienced early encounters with situations calling for considerable responsibility.

There is some evidence as well, although it is less potent, that those respondents who are both oldest and youngest are the most adversarial. More than six out of ten either under forty-one years of age or over fifty are relatively challenging, compared with only about four out of ten in their forties. There is also some evidence that being in the military reserves is related to an adversarial posture. The total effect of these factors, nevertheless, is not clear at this juncture (see Table 29).

Organizational Experience

Unlike those who challenge officials in the field, those who consider officials in Washington as adversaries are likely to enjoy a considerable amount of autonomy and to have followed solo professional career patterns. Regarding news organizations respondents have worked for the longest time, almost two-thirds (64 percent) of those *not* working for a wire service are adversarial, compared to only about half (46 percent) of those who have been working for a wire service. In particular, those who work for either *The New York Times* or the *Washington Post* are by far the most adversarial reporters: about eight out of ten (79 percent) of such journalists demonstrate strong tendencies toward adversarial perspectives.

Organizational autonomy from mass market considerations is paral-

TABLE 29   Capital Opposition by Birth Order, Sibling Number, and Age

		Birth Order		Sibling Number		
				Zero or		Three or
		First Born	Later Born	One	Two	More
		%	%	%	%	%
Capital	High	65	51	61	40	70
Adversary	Low	35	49	39	60	30
		(34)	(37)	(31)	(20)	(20)
		prob = .26		prob = .14		

		Age (in years)		
		40 or less	41–50	51 or More
		%	%	%
Capital	High	67	42	61
Adversary	Low	33	58	39
		(24)	(19)	(28)
		prob = .25		

leled by person autonomy as an employee among those who consider Washington officials as adversaries. Almost seven out of ten (68 percent) of those with little or no reported supervisor control over their output are adversarial, compared with only 45 percent of those who report strong supervisor control. Organizational and employee autonomy apart, most respondents who display strong adversarial orientations toward officials in Washington are likely to pursue "solo professional" career patterns.

Unlike those who challenge officials abroad, respondents who challenge officials in Washington are likely to have little managerial or editorial experience. About six out of ten (63 percent) who never gained any managerial experience in Latin America are adversarial, compared with only about four out of ten (38 percent) who did acquire such experience. Similarly, over six out of ten who currently spend little time in management activities are adversarial, compared with only about four out of ten (44 percent) who supervise five or more employees. In sum, those who have little field managerial experience, who edit very little, who have very few employee supervision responsibilities, and who spend most of their time reporting are all likely to be adversarial toward officials in Washington, D.C. (see Table 30).

A solo professional career pattern suggests something significant. As Johnstone, Slawski, and Bowman suggest in *The News People: A Sociological Portrait of American Journalists and Their Work* (1976), a journalist who pursues a solo professional career admires those who achieve excellence in investigative or analytic reporting more than he admires those who generate large audiences for news or who are efficient in meeting deadlines. Those who define their careers in terms of organizational achievement, however, are likely to value reaching large audiences and reaching them quickly because such goals enhance the economic interests of news organizations (p. 128). Solo professionals typically devote more attention to their duties as professional news gatherers than to the duties of professional news managers or marketers.

Yet displaying professional news-gathering career paths does not necessarily suggest a concommitant wealth of experience with crisis reporting in Latin America for most respondents with adversarial perspectives. Those who challenge officials in Latin America appear to have some experience with crisis reporting, but those likely to challenge officials in Washington have relatively little experience with crisis reporting, especially with reporting on the coup in Brazil in 1964, Castro's coming to power in Cuba in 1959, and the election of Salvador Allende in Chile in 1970. Despite their lack of experience, they nevertheless display confidence in recent crisis reporting. Those who believe that reporting on the election of Allende in Chile in 1970 was accomplished are likely to be adversarial toward officials in Washington. And those respondents who believe the performance record of their own organizations in reporting on crises in Latin America is improving are also

TABLE 30 Capital Opposition by Employing Organization, Autonomy, and Latin and Current Supervisory Experience

| Capital Adversary | Employing Organization | | | | Estimated Supervisor Control | |
| | Broad Market | Select Market | | | | |
	(Wire Service) %	(Major Dailies) %	(Major Weeklies) %	(N.Y. Times Wash. Post) %	Little or None Little or None %	Strong Strong %
High	46	57	50	79	68	45
Low	54	43	50	21	22	55
	(24)	(14)	(14)	(19)	(38)	(33)

prob = .16 prob = .12

| Capital Adversary | Supervisory Experience (Latin America) | | Number of Employees Supervised Currently | |
	None %	Same %	5 or Less %	6 or More %
High	63	38	62	44
Low	37	62	38	56
	(57)	(13)	(55)	(16)

prob = .10 prob = .20

likely to be adversarial toward Washington officials. In general, Washington adversaries express a clear preference for analytical and explanatory reporting in the crises in which they are familiar, in contrast with a preference for reporting which emphasizes speed, breadth, and accuracy.

Social Network Factors

Consistent with the pattern exhibited by challengers in Latin America itself, Washington adversaries are likely to make friends abroad not with correspondents but with other contacts they make locally. A full three-quarters (75 percent) of those who say friends abroad are primarily not correspondents (especially not U.S. correspondents) tend to be adversarial, compared with only four out of ten (42 percent) who claim correspondents as close friends. This independence of foreign correspondents from local correspondents extends to relying primarily on sources other than local newsmen as important contacts in daily reporting. Journalists likely to challenge officials in Washington are also likely to rely on government sources and foreign correspondents for much of their reporting.

The independence of these solo professionals, whether in pursuing careers that emphasize reporting achievement, or in remaining independent of other correspondents, appears rooted less in reporting experience than in personal preference. Washington adversaries are not among the very most experienced reporters. They tend to demonstrate middle levels of journalistic experience, having been journalists for fifteen to twenty-five years. They have even fewer years experience writing about Latin America. Those with less than eight years reporting on the region tend to be the most adversarial in Washington. They also tend to be people who began reporting on Latin America early, within three years of beginning their careers as journalists.

This lack of "old-timer" status among such respondents is apparent in their lack of experience in a variety of the world's regions. Washington challengers may have had prior experience in North Africa or prior or current experience in Central America. But they tend to have had little experience in East Asia/China or the Middle East, and they have relatively little professional reporting knowledge concerning the Bay of Pigs in 1961 or the Dominican crisis in 1965 (see Table 31).

Conclusions

Several similarities and contrasts are apparent in comparing respondents most likely to be adversarial toward officials in Latin America and in Washington, D.C. Consider similarities first.

TABLE 31 Capital Opposition by Crisis Reporting Evaluations, Field Friendships and Years Experience in Journalism and in Regional Reporting

		Estimated Direction of Own Organization's Crisis Reporting (Open-Ended)		Field Friendships	
		Worse or Same %	Better %	Other Correspondents %	Not Correspondents %
Capital Adversary	High	42	73	42	75
	Low	58	27	58	25
		(26)	(11)	(33)	(24)
		prob = .23	prob = .01		

	Years in Journalism			Years Reporting on Latin America		
	17 or less %	18–25 %	26 or More %	7 or less %	8–14 %	15 or More %
High	53	71	50	70	54	50
Low	47	29	50	30	46	50
	(15)	(24)	(32)	(23)	(24)	(22)
	prob = .27		prob = .37			

Both types of adversaries are to be found predominantly in two age groups: those under forty-one and those over fifty. Respondents in their forties at the time of the survey, 1978–1979, are least likely to be adversarial, most likely to feel collegial toward government officials. A possible explanation for this finding is that reporters in their forties belong to a special historical generation. A researcher might ask what historical epoch helped form the occupational and adult political perspectives of such journalists when they first entered the work force in their twenties. Those in their forties (between forty-one and fifty) in 1978–1979 were in their twenties in the period 1948–1958. That period constitutes, by any reasonable measure, the height of the Cold War period, during which citizens were encouraged to identify closely with the national government generally and with U.S. foreign policy in particular. Journalists undergoing formative adult learning in that period may have identified with government policy and officials quite closely, an experience that may have shaped later perspectives and may have become quite resistant to change.

It is clear that both types of challengers exhibit high levels of independence. Challengers in Latin America display a great deal of autonomy from other correspondents. Challengers in Washington display a great deal of autonomy both within their organization and at an early age, in that they are likely to have shouldered a great deal of responsibility in their families of origin. D.C. challengers also report that they are relatively independent of strong supervisor control in their daily work.

Both kinds of adversaries see improvement in their organization's performance in reporting on crises in Latin America. Adversaries in Latin America see a great contrast between reporting on Cuba in 1959 and reporting on Chile in 1970, and challengers in Washington, D.C., see broad improvement in crisis reporting in organizations for which they have worked longest. It is further evident that reporting on the election of Salvador Allende in Chile in 1970 appears to have been a critical event for both kinds of challengers. Both the challengers in Latin America and the nations' capital appear to have liked reporting on Chile in far greater proportion than they have appreciated reporting on other crises.

A final parallel may be one of the most important. Challengers tend to be found in substantial concentrations in two of the most well-known newspapers in the United States: *The New York Times* and the *Washington Post*. Those two papers appeal to selected audiences, unlike our major wire services, which endeavor to sell news to very broad audiences. The same two newspapers, in addition, exercise a substantial amount of influence in helping set foreign-policy agendas. With their influence and distinction they may, in ways difficult to measure, nurture and encourage those types of newsmen most likely to challenge officials.

Contrasts

For all the similarities, a few contrasts are apparent between challengers in Latin America and challengers in Washington, D.C. Adversaries abroad tend to follow careers in management more than those who challenge in the nation's capital. The latter are likely to pursue solo professional careers, admiring the achievements of news gatherers rather than the achievements of those who rise in the hierarchies of news organizations. Differences in prior experience are also apparent. Latin American adversaries display considerable regional experience reporting on the region, while challengers in Washington exhibit relatively little regional experience.

Several contrasts between adversaries and the examiners discussed in the previous chapter are apparent. Examiners are relatively young and lack autonomy in making news decisions. They are also relatively innocent of the progress made in acquiring explanatory and analytical respectives on reporting, progress evident to reporters who have been involved in professional journalism for a longer period of time. Adversaries, by contrast, whatever their levels of achievement, are more experienced. Further, adversaries are capable of appreciating changes in reporting performance over time and are likely to value coverage of the election of Allende in Chile in 1970 more highly than do the less-experienced examiners.

Contrasts apart, two parallels are striking. One is that neither examiners, perhaps for reasons of youth, nor adversaries, perhaps by preference, display high levels of friendship with Latin American nationals. Instead, examiners display considerable curiosity about Latin America as a region, while adversaries display considerable concern for journalism as a profession worthy of serious commitment in itself. A second similarity is significant. Both examiners and adversaries tend to work outside the major wire services. Examiners are likely to work outside such services, and adversaries are specifically found most likely to work for either the *Washington Post* or *The New York Times*. It is not clear at this juncture whether or not people who are already examining and adversarial tend to apply for positions at those news organizations, or whether, once hired, the news organizations inculcate special values in their recruits. Whatever the best explanation, it is clear that both types of professionals are in disproportionate numbers to be found working outside the major wire services.

6

Learning to Be a Pluralist

Pluralist And Hegemonic Perspectives On Political Change

Any investigation of professional learning among foreign correspondents is incomplete unless it explores the way journalists think about political change abroad. Whatever their views about reporting in general or their relations with government officials, any comprehensive portrait of the learning patterns of journalists cannot be drawn until their orientations or general perspectives on political change are clarified. This analysis identifies two such perspectives. Each one is quite possibly an extreme vision. Few people in the professional world of journalism may actually cling to either in its pure form. But the two perspectives present, if not a precise set of attitude categories for foreign correspondents, opposing tendencies all journalists may be compelled to consider under crisis conditions.

This study calls those two opposing perspectives "pluralist" and "hegemonic." A preference for political reporting that appreciates the potential of other countries for self government may view foreign political leaders as capable of autonomous innovation and growth, foreign political institutions as capable of functioning through the application of energy and talent, and cross national relations for foreign countries as opportunities for the exercise of national choices about trade, investment, diplomacy, and other in-teractions. This vision of international possibilities does not suggest that journalists brighten dismal political situations with hopes of civic participa-tion where little hope exists. Rather it is a perspective derived from the op-timism of the Enlightenment, exalting not the certainty, but the possibility, of egalitarian participation in political life. This "ideal-type" vision of political reporting, rooted in Eighteenth century intellectual currents (and shared in the North American colonies by the Founding Fathers), can be called a "pluralist" viewpoint, cherishing the capacity of citizens to par-ticipate in their own self-government and of nations to manage their own af-fairs with relative autonomy.

In sharp contrast to this vision is one which may be labeled a "hege-monic" perspective, (Pollock, 1978). It refers to an orientation that regards with suspicion efforts at change carried out without the guidance, or in de-fiance, of a Western industrialized country. A hegemonic vision is some-times apparent when developing countries, or classes or groups within them, attempt to change substantially their subordinate condition. A hegemonic perspective is quite different from its pluralist opposite. It may regard leaders calling for rapid change as "unrepresentative." It may view political institutions substantially different from our own as somewhat inaccessible to popular sentiment. And it may consider international relations exercised by countries calling for substantial change as being fraught with danger. But what most distinguishes the hegemonic perspective is the tendency to regard intervention abroad or conflict as a relatively natural or inevitable way to resolve differences.

What this study calls a hegemonic viewpoint is similar to what John Kenneth Galbraith in 1978 called "global strategic thought." (John Kenneth Galbraith, "the strategic mind," the *New York Review of Books* (October 12, 1978), p. 72.) Writing in the *New York Review of Books,* Galbraith ex-pressed concern that "global strategic thought sometimes called relentless strategic thought (is) again rampant in Washington. There is nothing of which the country should be more concerned," he said.

> President Carter can shrug off the odd prophesorial attack but recent experience shows that presidents cannot survive the strategic mind. If life on this planet dissolves one day in an intense sheet of flame, with great over-pressure, the guidance to our demise will have been given by a relentless strategic mind, a par-ticularly tough exponent of global balance.
>
> (The strategic mind is not) primarily concerned with weapons and weaponry. Rather it is drawn uncontrollably to any map of the world, and this it immediate-ly divides into spheres of present and potential influence.
>
> A hostile sphere of influence always requires a prompt and lethal reaction that is partly, it is held, because nothing else will be understood. And partly it is

because it must be shown that we are capable of such a reaction. Those who question the need and ask consideration of the consequences show by their insistence on thought that they are indecisive. The man of relentless strategic mind substitutes bravery for thought, action for reflection." (Galbraith, 1978: p. 72.)

To the extent U.S. involvement in Vietnam represents one example of the power of the strategic mind in powerful policy positions, journalists who value their tradition of examining and serving as watchdogs on abuses of political power are also likely to be concerned with the power of those who favor hegemonic, strategic policies. It is reasonable to assume that those journalists who are most opposed to such perspectives are also the same journalists most likely to favor a pluralist posture in world affairs. Journalists who value pluralism are not likely to witness casual efforts at intervention abroad without calling attention to their dangers. It is therefore useful for this investigation to examine why some journalists become more anti-hegemonic or more pluralist than others.

Orientations Toward Non-Intervention and Detente

In order to explore which journalists are most likely to become pluralists, two scales were constructed, one measuring a preference toward non-intervention in foreign affairs generally and in Third World countries in particular, the other measuring a preference for detente. Each scale was composed of several items. Both scales were tested to insure that each was unidimensional, fulfilling the criteria for Guttman scales.

Those who favor non-intervention are found to agree and disagree with the following statements:

We should cooperate fully with smaller democracies and not regard ourselves as their leaders. (Agree strongly, 52 percent)

Relinquishing the Panama Canal may reduce substantially the capacity of the U.S. to maintain peace in the hemisphere. (Disagree strongly, 62 percent)

When a national government is incompetent, the use of economic sanctions against it can be justified. (Uncertain, Disagree somewhat, or Disagree strongly, 79 percent)

When a national government is incompetent, the use of force to remove it can be justified. (Uncertain, Disagree somewhat, and Disagree strongly, 77 percent).[1]

Guttman scaling procedures reveal that journalists most likely to favor non-intervention hold several related opinions. They believe we should exercise more cooperation than leadership in international affairs, they believe that relinquishing the Panama Canal will not diminish U.S. national security, and they believe that the use of economic sanctions and force against other governments, however much we may disagree with them, is seldom justified.

Correspondents who favor non-intervention are similar to those who favor detente. Guttman scaling procedures reveal that the following items are strongly related to one another and measure a coherent preference for detente:

Military considerations play too great a role in formulating U.S. foreign policy. (Agree strongly, 17 percent)

Only a show of military strength can prevent the U.S.S.R. from trying to gain world domination. (Uncertain, Disagree somewhat, Disagree strongly, 52 percent)

The only way to maintain peace is to keep American so powerful and well-armed that no other nation will dare attack us. (Uncertain, Disagree somewhat, Disagree strongly, 57 percent)

The first principle of foreign policy should be to join forces with any country, even if it is not very democratic, just as long as it is strongly anti-Communist. (Disagree strongly, 69 percent).[2]

Scaling procedures reveal that journalists who favor detente believe that military considerations loom large in U.S. foreign policy, that military strength is not the only major weapon in our diplomatic arsenal, and that the United States should be wary of aligning itself with countries without strong democratic traditions.

Combining the responses of all the respondents into the two scales measuring preferences for non-intervention and detente, it is clear that about 50 percent are quite favorable toward non-intervention; while about 38 percent are similarly favorable to detente. It is also clear that the same journalists opposed to intervention abroad are highly likely to favor detente also (see Table 32).

Learning To Oppose Intervention

Respondents most likely to oppose intervention abroad tend to belong to a middle, perhaps middle-aged, occupational generation, to be high achievers, and to be solo professionals rather than managers.

Lifecycle Factors

"Oppositionists," or those who favor non-intervention, are most likely to be found in the age group between forty-one and fifty. Oppositionists are therefore precisely in the very group least likely to be examining or adver-

TABLE 32

	Non-Intervention %		Detente %
Most Favorable	50.5	Most Favorable	37.5
Very Favorable	29	Very Favorable	23
Somewhat Favorable	20.4	Somewhat Favorable	26
and Least Favorable		Least Favorable	13.5
	(93)		(96)

		Detente		
		Low %	Medium %	High %
	High	31.4	52	66
Non-Intervention	Medium	34.3	19	23
	Low	34.3	29	11
		(35)	(21)	(35)
	prob = .05			

sarial. Whatever their ages, people concerned about intervention report majoring in subjects that emphasize individual expression over an interest in groups. About six out of ten humanities and journalism majors are non-interventionists, compared with only about a quarter (27 percent) of social-science majors. Unlike examiners, however, those opposed to intervention tend to stop their formal education at bachelor's degrees.

Early humanism is possibly reinforced by the character of military experience. Those without any military experience at all are likely to oppose intervention. About eight out of ten who have not experienced military service are non-interventionists, compared with a little over two-thirds who have seen military service. Among those who have been exposed to the military, however, those with the most experience appear strongly against intervention. Two-thirds who have been in the military and have served on active duty for three or more years are strongly against intervention, compared with only about four out of ten who have served for less than three years (see Table 33).

Organizational Factors

The organizational experience of non-interventionists suggests they exhibit the classic career patterns of solo professionals. They tend to have less than the highest salaries, typically collecting an annual salary of less than $38,000. They also exhibit little or no managerial experience, operating as individuals. Inside Latin America, they appear to have had little editing experience, and most of them spent all their time reporting. Consistent with their lack of managerial experience, they report that in their current position they have very little authority over the hiring and firing of others employed at the same news organization (see Table 34).

TABLE 33   Non-Intervention by Age, College Major and Military Experience

| | | Age | | |
| | | 40 or Less | 41 – 50 | 51 or More |
		%	%	%
Non- Intervention	High	44	62	46
	Medium	56	38	54
	or Low	(34)	(24)	(35)
	prob = .47			

| | | College Major | | |
| | | Social Sciences | Humanities | Journalism |
		%	%	%
Non- Intervention	High	27	59	58
	Medium	73	41	42
	or Low	(22)	(32)	(24)
	prob = .11			

	Highest Degree			Active Military Duty	
				One or two years	Three years or More
	B.A.	M.A.			
	%	%		%	%
Non- Intervention	High 55	33 High		44	67
	Medium 45	67 Medium		56	33
	or Low (60)	(21) or Low		(23)	(24)
	prob = .16	prob = .22			

Not only do non-interventionists follow solo professional career patterns, they also appear quite conscious of their preference for occupational autonomy. Seven out of ten who report that they operate mostly as autonomous individuals in their work are opposed to intervention, compared with only about four out of ten who believe they are more integrated into news organizations, operating as members of a team. This does not suggest that solo professionals are unstable in their career patterns, because non-interventionists are found almost equally among those who worked very few years for the same organization or among those who have worked the most years for the same organization. About half of those who have worked ten or fewer years with the same news organizations and about half who have worked eighteen or more years with the same organizations are likely to oppose intervention (see Table 35).

Network Factors
When their friendshp network patterns are examined, non-interventionists are found least among the most-experienced reporters, but they also display abundant self-reliance and autonomy. Those with fewer than twenty-six or

TABLE 34   Non-Intervention by Salary, Editing Experience in Latin America, and Personnel Influence

| | | | Highest Annual | |
		Less than $27,500	$27,000 – $37,000	More than $37,500
		%	%	%
Non-Intervention	High	53	54	38
	Medium or Low	47	46	62
		(32)	(35)	(26)
	prob = .03			

| | | Editing Experience in Latin America (In Percent of Time) | | |
		None		Some
		%	%	
Non-Intervention	High	56		33
	Medium or Low	44		67
		(66)		(24)
	prob = .11			

| | | Self-Reported Influence Over Hiring and Firing | |
		Small	Large
		%	%
Non-Intervention	High	58	30
	Medium or Low	42	70
		(66)	(27)
	prob = .04		

more years of reporting experience and those who began reporting on Latin America since Sputnik (during the last twenty-three years) are more likely to be opposed to intervention than colleagues who are more experienced and who graduated and began reporting on Latin America prior to 1957.

Self-reliance is also a hallmark of non-interventionists. They remain aloof from business executives and from other journalists. They have few professional memberships. About six out of ten who hold no memberships in professional journalism societies are opposed to intervention, compared with only about four out of ten who are members of professional societies (see Table 36).

The autonomy and self-reliance displayed by journalists in their friendship and membership networks parallels a tendency to refrain from involvement in their countries of assignment. Non-interventionists tend to be familiar with fewer languages than those who regard intervention more kindly and report their best friends are not nationals of countries. In addition, those opposed to intervention tend to rely primarily on foreign sources, involving

TABLE 35   Non-Intervention by Term Context and Longevity with a Single Employer

		Team Work Context	
		Individual %	Team (At least 50% of Time) %
Non-Intervention	High	71	41
	Medium or Low	29	59
		(28)	(61)
	prob = .03		

		Largest Number of Years Worked For a Single News Organization		
		10 or Fewer %	11 – 17 %	18 or More %
Non-Intervention	High	55	39	55
	Medium or Low	45	61	45
		(33)	(28)	(31)
	prob = .22			

TABLE 36   Non-Intervention by Years of Experience Reporting on Latin America and Professional Participation

		Number of Years Experience Reporting on Latin America		
		7 or Less %	8 – 14 %	15 or More %
Non-Intervention	High	63	40	43
	Medium or Low	37	60	57
		(33)	(30)	(28)
	prob = .24			

		Professional Membership	
		None %	One or More %
Non-Intervention	High	57	39
	Medium or Low	43	61
		(42)	(44)
	prob = .14		

themselves somewhat less with local government and non-government sources of news. Oppositionists display considerable distance from involvement in their countries of assignment (see Table 37).

Consistent with their somewhat recent involvement in foreign affairs re-

TABLE 37   Non-Intervention by Knowledge of Non-Iberian Languages, Field Friendships, and Source Preferences

| | | Conversational Familiarity with Non-Iberian Languages | | |
| | | None | One | Two or More |
		%	%	%
Non-Intervention	High	54	59	32
	Medium	46	41	68
	or Low	(37)	(29)	(25)

| | | Best Friends When Posted in Latin America | |
| | | From Latin America | From the United States |
		%	%
Non-Intervention	High	42	54
	Medium	58	46
	or Low	(41)	(39)

prob = .11

| | | Preferred Local Sources | | |
| | | Foreign Diplomats and Correspondents | Local Officials | Local Non-Officials |
		%	%	%
Non-Intervention	High	60	47	43
	Medium	40	53	57
	or Low	(15)	(30)	(28)

prob = .11

porting and the distance they maintain from critical events abroad, few non-interventionists have reporting experience in South or Southeast Asia or North Africa. They also are very unlikely to have professional experience in reporting on two of the major East-West critical events occurring in Latin America, the ascension of power of Fidel Castro in Cuba in 1959, and the election of Salvador Allende in Chile in 1970. Considered altogether, the chief characteristics of non-interventionists — their less than long-term involvement in reporting, their distance from other journalists and nationals in their countries of assignment, and their lack of involvement in their own news organizations or crisis reporting on Latin America — all support the proposition that there is a clear parallel between the personal and occupational orientations of reporters and their perspectives on U.S. intervention abroad. Wishing little interference in their own lives and their own definition of their work, reporters opposed to intervention abroad maintain a consistent pattern opposing intervention both in their own lives and in the affairs of other countries as well.

Learning To Support East-West Pluralism

Those correspondents who can be considered pluralists because they favor detente are similar to those who oppoose intervention in some ways and different in others. Those who favor non-intervention and detente tend to be humanities majors and, in the case of non-interventionists, may be journalism majors as well. Respondents with both orientations tend to earn middle-level annual salaries of between $28,000 and $38,000 and, to a somewhat lesser extent, smaller salaries. Both value autonomy greatly. Both groups believe they work more as individuals than as people integrated into team efforts. In both cases, respondents basically like their own organizations and would enjoy continuing to work for them.

Both those who oppose intervention and those who favor detente appear to occupy some middle levels of experience and achievement in the world of foreign correspondents. Neither group is among the very most experienced reporters. Respondents in both groups tend to have less than twenty-six years experience reporting, with those who favor detente displaying somewhat more reporting experience, belonging more often to the fifteen- to twenty-year range. Finally, as is the case for those who tend to be examiners or adversaries, both groups report few friends among the nationals of the country where they are stationed.

Beyond the similarities, however, there are many differences between those who hold orientations opposing intervention or favoring detente. Respondents favoring detente tend to have shouldered a considerable amount of responsibility both in their families of origin and their families of choice and tend to be relatively well-educated. Regarding organizational experience, those favoring detente, although autonomous, tend to have more supervisory responsibilities, and they also tend to have spent relatively few years with any single news organization. Those favoring detente are relatively mobile and managerial rather than solo professional in their career patterns.

Regarding the friendship and source networks of those favoring detente, they tend to have less experience reporting on Latin America than do those who are opposed to intervention, and they also tend to have a broader circle of friends than non-interventionists, relying somewhat less on other journalists for close friendships and displaying cosmopolitan interests. They also tend to place primary reliance on sources in the local government they contact, whereas non-interventionists tend to rely primarily on foreign sources for their news material. One of the major differences significant for this study, however, is the difference the two groups display in the way they think about the reporting profession generally. Those who favor detente are highly likely to display an examining posture toward the journalism profession generally, whereas those opposed to intervention are much less likely to be either examiners or non-interventionists.

Lifecycle Factors

Some age or generational factors are related to favoring detente, but educational factors and family factors, measuring family responsibilities, appear even more strongly related to East-West orientations. Those who belong to generations graduating since Sputnik was launched in 1957 tend to favor detente more than those who graduated prior to that period. Over four out of ten who graduated after 1957 favor detente, compared with only three out of ten who graduated prior to that. Consistently, an examination of age groups reveals that younger reporters forty or younger are more likely to favor detente than those who are older. Three-quarters of those forty or younger favor detente compared to about half of those who are older (see Table 38).

Educational factors are more clearly linked to attitudes toward detente than are generational factors. About six out of ten journalists (57 percent) with Master's degrees favor detente, compared to only about four out of ten (38 percent) who have bachelors' degrees. Regarding college majors or areas of concentration in college, those who majored in a humanities discipline are most likely to favor detente, followed by journalists. Social scientists are least likely to favor detente. It is striking, in addition, that most journalists who attended non-elite colleges are far more likely than their more-privileged colleagues to cherish detente. Almost half (49 percent) of those who attended non-elite colleges view detente positively, compared to only about one-third (36 percent) who attended either major state universities or elite private institutions of higher learning (see Table 39).

Although educational experience is strongly associated with detente, family experiences are also potent factors. Family experiences may have little to do with whether or not a respondent favors or opposes intervention, but correspondents valuing detente highly are likely not to be first-born in their

TABLE 38 Favoring Detente by College Generation

		Year Graduated Pre-Sputnik %	From College Post-Sputnik %
Favoring Detente	High	36	46
	Medium or Low	64	54
		(36)	(46)
	prob = .14		

TABLE 39 Favoring Detente by Age, Educational Level, College Major, and College Status

		Age			Master's Degree	
		40 or Less %	41 – 50 %	More than 50 %	No %	Yes %
Favoring Detente	High or Medium	75	50	55	38	57
	Low	25 (35)	50 (28)	45 (33)	62 (61)	43 (21)

prob = .20   prob = .20

		College Major			Status of College	
		Social Sciences %	Humanities %	Journalism %	Non-Elite %	Elite %
Favoring Detente	High or Medium	33	48	40	49	36
	Low	67 (21)	52 (33)	60 (25)	51 (41)	64 (42)

prob = .35   prob = .19

families of origin, yet have very few siblings. Almost half (49 percent) of those who were first-born are likely to favor detente, compared to only 29 percent who were born after the first child in their family. Similarly, over four out of ten respondents in families where there are few children (ranging from an only child to three children in total) are likely to favor detente, compared to only two out of ten respondents in families where there are four or more children. Among those who consider detente important, early sibling experiences are likely to encourage the early development of a sense of self-sufficiency and responsibility, either for oneself or one's small family.

Marital status, associated with a respondent's family of choice, is also strikingly related to a preference for detente. Half of those who are *not* married to an original spouse — that is, people who are single, divorced, widowed, separated, or remarried — value detente highly. By contrast, only three out of ten (32 percent) of those who are still married to their original spouse favor detente. Perhaps the personal experience of either being alone or suffering loss engenders an appreciation for the importance of peace, both in the personal family and in the family of nations (see Table 40).

Organizational Factors

The organizational experience of those who prefer detente represents a personal history of at least modest achievement, managerial experience, and both organizational and personal autonomy.

About half of those who have middle-level salaries, making between $28,000 and $38,000 annually, favor detente. By contrast, three out of ten with lower salaries, and two out of ten with higher salaries, do so. In addition to middle-level salaries, those who prefer detente tend to have high managerial rank and experience. Most supervise one to five employees and about a third supervise six or more employees. Only about a quarter supervise no employees at all. Consistent with supervisory experience, journalists who are engaged in some amount of editing currently are more likely to favor detente than are those with little editing experience (see Table 41).

Along with their achievements, respondents valuing detente are likely to believe they are extraordinarily autonomous. About half believe they are extraordinarily autonomous. About half believe they operate as individuals most of the time, and only about a third believe they operate as a member of a team in producing news material. Some evidence for autonomy is apparent in the discovery that detente supporters have been employed by a single news organization for only a few years. Almost five out of ten of those who favor detente have been with their news organizations only a relatively short time, less than eleven years, whereas only about one-third of those who have been with their news organizations a longer period of time similarly favor detente.

Personal autonomy is also paralleled by some organizational autonomy in the news marketplace. Examiners and adversaries tend to work far less

TABLE 40 Favoring Detente by Birth Order, Number of Siblings, and Marital Stability

| | Birth Order | | Number of Siblings | | |
	Born After First Child %	First Born %	Only Child or 1 Sibling %	2 Siblings %	Three or More Siblings %
Favoring Detente High	29	47	46	44	20
Medium or Low	71	53	54	56	80
	(49)	(47)	(43)	(23)	(30)
	prob = .15	prob = .16			

| | Marital Stability | |
	Married to First Spouse %	Not Married or Not Married to First Spouse %
Favoring Detente High	32	50
Medium or Low	68	50
	(66)	(30)
	prob = .22	

TABLE 41 Favoring Detente by Salary and Supervisory Authority

		Highest Annual Salary (in dollars)		
		Less than $27,500	$27,500 - $37,499	$37,500 and More
		%	%	%
Favoring Detente	High	33	53	22
	Medium or Low	67	47	78
		(33)	(36)	(27)

prob = .09

		Number of Employees Supervised		
		None	1 - 5	6 or More
		%	%	%
Favoring Detente	High	30	56	39
	Medium or Low	70	44	69
		(43)	(23)	(23)

prob = Not available

frequently for wire services than for other news organizations. A similar tendency is true for those who favor detente, but to a lesser degree. About four out of ten respondents who do not work for wire services are likely to value detente, whereas three out of ten who work for wire services do so. This difference is not very large. Those who oppose intervention, for example, are equally likely to be found inside or outside the wire services. Regarding support for detente outside of the wire services, those who support detente are about equally likely to be found in any of the other types of news organizations: major news weeklies, *The New York Times,* or the *Washington Post,* or the other major papers included in this study (see Table 42).

Organizational autonomy apart, personal autonomy is expressed in the dissonance some respondents express in evaluating crisis coverage printed by their own news organizations. Those who are relatively critical of coverage of Castro's accession to power in Cuba in 1959, the military coup in Brazil in 1964, and coverage of Chilean elections in 1970 are likely to support detente (see Table 43).

Compared to those who oppose intervention, respondents who support detente tend to have more supervisory and managerial experience. They also tend to be less tied to particular news organizations. Those who value detente tend to have relatively little experience in any single news organization, but those who oppose intervention display either very few or a great many years working for the same news organization.

TABLE 42 Favoring Detente by Teamwork Context, Organizational Stability, and Employing News Organization

	Teamwork Context		Longest Years Worked for Same Organization		
	Individual %	50% or Greater Teamwork %	10 or Less %	11–17 %	18 or More %
Favoring Detente — High	48	34	47	36	31
Medium or Low	52	66	53	64	69
	(31)	(62)	(32)	(31)	(32)

prob = .29   prob = .19

	Employing News Organization			Employing News Organization			
	Broad Market (Wire Services) %	Select Market (Other) %		Wire Services %	Major Dailies %	Weeklies %	N.Y. Times Wash. Post %
High	31	43		31	44	41	43
Medium or Low	69	57		69	56	59	57
	(42)	(54)		(42)	(16)	(17)	(21)

prob = .18   prob = .25

118

TABLE 43   Favoring Detente by Evaluation of Organizational Performance on Chile (1970)

| | | News Organization Performance on Chile 1970 | |
| | | Fair or Poor | Outstanding or Good |
		%	%
Favoring	High	50	33
Detente	Medium or Low	50	67
		(16)	(45)
	prob = .25		

Network Factors

Most of those who favor detente have curiously little experience in reporting on Latin America and only moderate experience in reporting generally. About half of those who have less than eight years reporting on the region support detente, whereas only about a third of those who have reported on the region for a longer period do so.

Regional experience apart, almost half of those who have worked in journalism for fifteen to twenty-five years support detente, and about a third who have worked for fewer than fifteen years also support it. But only a quarter of those who have worked in journalism a longer time, more than twenty-five years, favor detente. Most of those who consider detente important have begun reporting on Latin America recently since the Tet offensive in Vietnam in 1968. They exhibit middle levels of experience in journalism; they are by no means the most experienced journalists.

Moderate professional longevity apart, most supporters of detente identify with journalism as a serious craft and are likely to like the organizations they work for. Almost five out of ten of those who would like to remain working at the same organization after five years favor detente, compared to only 14 percent of those who would prefer working elsewhere (see Table 44).

Supporting detente is associated with less experience reporting on Latin America than is an orientation opposing intervention. Most respondents who consider non-intervention to be important have been reporting on Latin America since Sputnik (1957), in contrast to those who espouse detente, who have typically been reporting on the region since about 1968. The two orientations are found to be distinct in another respect as well. Those who oppose intervention believe they are relatively autonomous from government officials and business executives and are likely to consider other journalists their closest friends. Those who support detente, by contrast, are rather likely nor unlikely to consider journalists their close friends.

For example, those pluralists who endorse detente have somewhat less respect for U.S. colleagues reporting from Latin America than for U.S. correspondents generally. Four out of ten who judge their colleagues reporting

TABLE 44   Favoring Detente by Experience in Journalism, Reporting on Latin America, and Satisfaction with Work

| | | Reporting on Latin America (in years) | | |
		7 or Less %	8 - 14 %	15 or More %
Favoring	High	53	24	33
Detente	Medium or Low	47	76	67
		(34)	(33)	(27)
	prob = .02			

| | | Journalism Experience (in years) | | |
		17 or Less %	18 - 25 %	26 or More %
Favoring	High	36	50	27
Detente	Medium or Low	64	50	73
		(25)	(34)	(37)
	prob = .05			

| | | Preferred Occupation After Five Years | |
		Outside Same Organization %	Inside Same Organization %
Favoring	High	14	46
Detente	Medium or Low	32	18
		(28)	(55)
	prob = .02		

for the region as below average or otherwise lacking, favor detente, compared to only three out of ten who consider their regional colleagues superior to reporters covering other regions for major U.S. news outlets.

Journalists with a detente orientation are not only distant from colleagues, they are also very little integrated into friendship networks with local citizens. Over four out of ten who believe Latin American news has received too little attention from supervisors support detente, compared to only about one-third who believe that their supervisors give Latin America just the right amount of attention. Yet supporters of detente claim very few Spanish- or Portuguese-speaking friends. Over four out of ten who have very few Latin American friends support detente, compared to only about three out of ten who say many or most of their friends are Latin Americans.

Despite their distance from other journalists and Latin Americans generally, supporters of detente are relatively cosmopolitan. While non-interventionists rely mainly on foreign correspondents and foreign government sources for news material, supporters of detente are equally likely to rely on foreign sources and local government sources. Correspondents concerned about detente are also likely to have at least a few business executives as friends, in contrast with those who oppose intervention. In addition, while non-interventionists have little familiarity with foreign languages, those who endorse detente tend to be familiar with at least one other foreign language in addition to Spanish and Portuguese (see Table 45).

Cosmopolitan perspectives apart, supporters of detente manifest the same lack of experience in crisis reporting in Latin America and elsewhere in the world that is evident among non-interventionists. Perhaps because of their recency in regional reporting, detente supporters are not professionally familiar with reporting on Cuba in 1959 or the Bay of Pigs crisis in 1961. In addition, they tend to report no prior professional experience reporting from North Africa or Sub-Saharan Africa, and they are most likely to lack experience in reporting from East Asia or China. This lack of experience in reporting on critical events on Latin America or elsewhere suggests that those who favor detente, unlike those who oppose intervention, may not have developed extensive contacts with sources inside or outside journalism who are experienced in crisis reporting.

Similarities and Differences

This examination of pluralism among foreign correspondents has focused on two types of pluralists, those who oppose intervention abroad generally and those who oppose East-West conflict in particular. Several parallels are

TABLE 45. Favoring Detente by Friendships with Other Journalists, Host Country Nationals and Familiarity with New Iberian Languages

		Friendships with Host Country Nationals	
		Few %	Many or Most %
Favoring	High	15	30
Detente	Medium or Low	66	70
		(33)	(54)
	prob = .08		

		Non-Iberian Familiar Languages		
		None %	One %	Two or More %
Favoring	High	32	50	27
Detente	Medium or Low	68	50	73
		(38)	(30)	(26)
	prob = .34			

found between the types of respondents who favor both pluralistic perspectives, but the differences between the two types of reporters may be more significant than the similarities.

Among the similarities between those who oppose intervention and those who oppose East-West conflict are the following: majoring in one of the humanities; high achievement (middle-level salaries); feeling autonomous within news organizations; liking the organization one works for; having few friends among Latin American nationals; less than twenty-six years experience as a journalist; and lack of experience in crisis reporting.

Among the differences between non-interventionists and those who favor detente:

Lifecycle Factors

Those in favor of detente tend to be first-born, are from small families, and
   are not married to their original spouses.
Those favoring detente tend to be among the youngest correspondents, although those most for detente are found among all ages. Non-interventionists tend to be in their forties.
Supporters of detente tend to have Master's degrees, in contrast to those who
   oppose intervention.
Those opposed to intervention tend to have no military experience, or if they
   do have it, have a great deal of it.
Anti-interventionists also tend to claim small towns or cities as their points
   of origin.

Organizational Factors

Non-interventionists claim little managerial experience and follow solo professional careers, whereas supporters of detente display considerable
   experience with supervisory experience;
Organizational stability: supporters of detente have relatively little experience in any single news organization, whereas those opposed to intervention stay very few or a great many years in a single place.
Working outside a wire-service organization: supporters of detente tend
   somewhat to work outside of wire services, whereas those opposed to
   intervention are equally likely to work in any kind of news organization.

Network Factors

Experience in reporting on Latin America: non-interventionists are likely to
   have reported on the region for a relatively long period, since 1957,
   whereas supporters of detente are likely to have reported on the region
   only since 1968.

Friendship patterns: non-interventionists are more likely to have U.S. journalists as friends than are supporters of detente, who are somewhat
critical of their U.S. colleagues; non-interventionists have few or no executive friends, whereas supporters of detente have at least some.

Sources: non-interventionists tend to rely on foreign sources, whereas supporters of detente rely equally on foreign and on local sources in their
country of assignment for information.

World interests: non-interventionists tend to speak few languages other than
Spanish or Portuguese. Supporters of detente tend to speak at least one
language other than an Iberian one.

Notes

1. The full list of "non-intervention" items is found in the survey questionnaire. That list is
composed of items selected from already validated scales described in Levinson 1957; Lutzker
1960; and Campbell 1960; described in Robinson, et. al., 1968.

2. The full list of "detente" items is found in the survey questionnaire (Appendix I). That list
is composed of items selected from already validated scales described in Levinson 1957;
Lutzker 1960, and Campbell 1960; described in Robinson, et. al., 1968.

PART THREE

7

Becoming a Correspondent
Several Types of Professionals

Previous chapters have described a broad array of factors affecting the development of professional perspectives in foreign correspondents. Many different experiences appear associated with learning to be an examiner, an adversary, and a pluralist. What previous chapters do not attempt to accomplish, however, is to compare the factors that predict professionalism with one another, focusing on only the most significant. A standard technique, called factor analysis, is employed to reduce the number of significant factors to only those capable of making the most powerful contribution to the acquisition of professional orientations. That analysis, in turn, permits the identification of clusters of factors associated with professionalism and facilitates learning about several distinct types of reporters likely to demonstrate high levels of professionalism under crisis conditions.

Challenging Prevailing Wisdom

The following analysis is more than an academic exercise in data comparison and factor reduction. It yields clear conclusions that are strikingly at odds with a number of conventional assumptions often made about the beliefs and behavior of foreign affairs reporters. Some of those popular assumptions include the following:

A new, younger generation of journalists is responsible for most of the "adversarial" reporting evident in foreign affairs reporting since the Vietnam period.

The more experienced a reporter is in his occupation, the more "professional" he is likely to be.

The more knowledge a reporter gains about a region, the more professional he is likely to become.

The more friendships a journalist enjoys with nationals of the host country, the more professional his reporting is likely to be.

The types of sources a journalist contacts frequently have a great influence on his professional orientations.

Each of the preceding assumptions represent a common set of attitudes toward the practice of foreign affairs reporting. Each is challenged in the following analysis.

Several Distinct Types

In order to explore the way different factors cluster in their association with professional perspectives, a factor analysis was completed for each of the examining, adversarial, and pluralist measures. In this kind of simple kind of factor analysis, the major factors associated with each perspective are correlated with one another in such a way that between one and five distinct columns of strongly associated factors emerge. Each column makes a precise contribution, or factor "loading," to the professional perspective under examination. Within each column, each factor makes a precise contribution to the overall column (the precise corollations between each factor and column are described in Appendix II).

Employing this method, between two and five types of journalists are found associated with each professional orientation. The accompanying tables illustrate the specific factors associated with each column-cluster, and the number found with each cluster indicates how strongly associated that cluster of factors is with the perspective under examination.

In this section, a term is introduced that deserves some explanation. Previous chapters have referred to "solo professionals" as a group distinct from "managers" or "organizational" people. Solo professionals have been described as reporters who occupy, or have occupied for many years, positions calling for the exercise of excellence in writing and gathering, as opposed to editing and managing, news. The factor-analysis technique employed in this chapter suggests that a further distinction is necessary.

Some journalists may pursue excellence in writing and news gathering, and can be considered excellent "craftsmen" (assuming that term describes both genders). Yet the same journalists may not be unusually "professional" because they may not: (a) have pursued a course of study leading to a Master's degree in journalism; or (b) be members of at least one "professional" association; or (c) believe that professional journalism societies should exercise greater authority over their membership; or, finally, (d) display some of the orientations described as "professional" in this study of foreign affairs reporters. Since these considerations — referring to educational level, association membership, association authority, and occupational codes and guidelines — encompass a good deal of what is commonly and historically considered "professional," a distinct term is required to describe someone who simply takes pride in excellent news gathering and writing. "Solo craftsman" can be used for that purpose because it connotes excellence and pride in carrying to completion a specific task, in this case a well written news product.

The five distinct perspectives examined in the study and the clusters associated with each can be listed briefly. For each perspective, the clusters are listed in rank-order (the most powerful first, the second most powerful second, etc.). Within each cluster, individual factors are also listed in rank order, with the most powerful first. (All factors correlate with the cluster loading with a value of at least .40, accounting for at least 16 percent of the variance for that cluster.)

Four Types of Examiners

High Examiner A: a solo craftsman writer, with group sharing experience acquired early in life (many siblings).

High Examiner B: Early responsibility (few siblings); current occupational group work; well-educated.

Low Examiner A: Experienced; no advanced degree; current occupational group work.

Low Examiner B: Many regional friends; solo craftsman writer.

(See Table 46)

Five Types of Field Adversaries

High Field Adversary A: Experienced; believes region unappreciated.

High Field Adversary B: Identifies with journalism craft and friendships; young; believes region unappreciated.

Low Field Adversary A: Managerial; friendly with colleagues.

Low Field Adversary B: Member of one or more professional societies; in work experience, a solo craftsman.

TABLE 46 Four Types of Examiners

	High Examiner A	High Examiner B	Low Examiner A	Low Examiner B
Factor Loading	(.64)*	(.32)	(−.42)	(−.26)
Significant Factors	A full-time reporter (No current editing activities)** Many siblings	Few siblings Team work context Master's Degree	Many years as a journalist Younger or older (not in 40's) No Master's Degree Teamwork context	Many Latin Full-time reporting (no editing)
Column Summary Description	Solo craftsman; early group experience	Early self-reliance; occupational group work; well educated	Experienced; current occupational group work	Many regional friends; solo craftsman

Total variance accounted for by five factors: .78
(Fifth factor has a .16 loading).

*The number under each column heading is the correlation between that entire factor and the orientation studied, in this case, an examining orientation.

**All items mentioned have at least a .40 correlation with each column's factor loading. Putting it another way, each item accounts for at least 16% of the variance in each column.

Low Field Adversary C: Works for a broad market news organization; vocational.

(See Table 47)

Four Types of Capital Adversaries

High Capital Adversary A: works for a daily weekly magazine and demonstrates a "solo professional," as opposed to a managerial, career track, supervising a few people.

High Capital Adversary B: the chief characteristic of this type is self-reliance tending to be first born, autonomous in his work role, with little managerial field experience and considerable optimism about the future of press performance; a self-reliant individual performer.

TABLE 47 Five Types of Field Adversaries

High Field A (.47)		High Field B (.23)
Many years writing about Latin America		Many journalist friends
Older or in 40's		Somewhat young or in 40's
Praised coverage of Chilean election in 1970		Supervisors little interested in the region (Latin America)
Familiar with Chilean election		
Supervisors little interested in region (Latin America)		
Experienced; believes region unappreciated		Identify with journalism profession and friendships; young; believes region unappreciated

Low Field A (-.47)	Low Field B (-.32)	Low Field C (-.27)
Editing experience in Latin America	Member of several professional associations	Work for a wire service
Many journalist friends	Journalism or Humanities major	Liked coverage of Chile
	Supervise few employees	No Master's degree
		Little travel outside of capital
		Journalism or Humanities major
Managerial; friendly with colleagues	Joins professional societies; otherwise, a skilled craftsman	Broad market; vocational

Total variance accounted for: .67

High Capital Adversary C: this adversary tends to have many brothers and sisters, is not first born, and has a number of friends in Latin America, and therefore has considerable group experience.

High Capital Adversary D: has current supervisory and field managerial experience, along with many Latin American friends. He follows a managerial career track and is interested in Latin America.

(See Table 48)

Four Types of Non-Interventionists

High Non-Interventionist A: a solo humanist vocational perspective; military exposure.

Low Non-Interventionist A: professionally active; successful; curious about region.

Low Non-Interventionist B: experienced, successful.

Low Non-Interventionist C: curious about region; friends and sources are distinct; less successful; group work context.

(See Table 49)

TABLE 48   Four Types of Capital Adversaries

High Capital A (.54)	High Capital B (.32)
Select market (daily newspaper or weekly magazine employer) (not a wire service)	First born
Few people supervised (solo craftsman)	Optimism about future press performance
	Little managerial field experience
	Little teamwork
Select market employer solo craftsman	Early adult self-reliance

High Capital C (.26)	High Capital D (.20)
Many siblings	Supervisory experience
Not first born	Field managerial experience
Best friends are Latin American	Best friends are Latin American
Early group experience; curiosity about region	Managerial; experience in the field and currently; curiosity about the region

Total variances accounted for by all five factors: 50

TABLE 49   Four Types of Non-Interventionists

High Non-Interventionist A (.64)	Low Non-Interventionist A (–.32)
Major in humanities or journalism Full time field reporter (little editing experience in Latin America Several years military service No Master's degree	Member of professional societies High salary Best friends are Latin American
Solo craftsman perspective; considerable military experience	Professionally active, successful, curious about region

Low Non-Interventionist B (–.30)	Low Non-Interventionist C (–.20)
Middle-aged (40's) Many years with the same organization Many years witing about Latin America High salary	Best friends are Latin American Prefer foreign over host-country sources Low salary Team work context
Experienced, successful	Friends and sources are distinct; less successful; current group experience

Total amount of variance accounted for by five factors: .64

Two Types of East-West Pluralists

High Pluralist: self-reliance in childhood and adult experience.
Low Pluralist: broad market employer; considerable experience in writing about the region, in the same organization, in a team work context; vocational.

(See Table 50)

The preceding array of types, or typology, presents a description of foreign affairs correspondents rich in their diversity and capable of starting at different points and arriving at the same attitudinal place — specifically, the adoption of professional perspectives on foreign affairs reporting. The variety in this typology pays tribute to the diverse backgrounds, experiences, and attitudes of foreign correspondents reporting on Latin America. Examining this richness more carefully, it is possible to isolate some factors as being more important than others and to compose a short list of observations found in this catalogue of foreign correspondent value patterns.

TABLE 50   Two Types of East-West Pluralists

High (.55)	Low (−.49)
Few Latin Friends	Employed by a wire service
Few siblings	Team work context
	Many years with the same organization
	Many years writing about Latin America
	No Master's degree
Self-reliance in childhood and adult experience	Broad market employer; considerable experience with group work, with the same employer, and with regional reporting.

Total amount of variance explained by all five factors: .60

Major Experiences Associated with Professional Perspectives

The identification of several types of reporters likely to hold professional orientations toward journalism permits further identification of those aspects of reporter life cycles, news organization experience, and friendship experience most conducive to learning professional orientations. The same typology also permits researchers to place to one side, if not disregard, a number of factors commonly thought associated with professionalism, but which this advanced comparative finds of little importance. Consider the significant factors first. A small set of learning experiences are linked to the acquisition of professional perspective on reporting.

Among Lifecycle Experiences, Preoccupational Experience Appears Quite Important

For example, being first-born is associated with an adversarial perspective in the nation's capital, and having few siblings is associated with a preference for East-West pluralism and for one type of examiner. Both the experience of being first-born or having few siblings is likely to encourage early learning in self-direction and responsibility, and that learning may help a reporter remain comfortable with independent judgments in adulthood.

Major in college is also somewhat associated with professional prospectives, although in a curious way. Social science majors tend to be more adversarial in the field, in Latin America, yet the same majors tend to regard

TABLE 51 Characteristics of Different Types of Professionals

Examiner	Field Adversary	Capital Adversary	Non-Interventionist	Detente (East-West Pluralist)
Solo craftsman; early group experience	Experienced; believes region unappreciated	Select market employer; solo craftsman	Solo craftsman; considerable military experience	Self-reliance in childhood and adulthood
Early self-reliance; occupational group experience; well-educated (identify with journalism profession)	Identify with journalism profession and friendships; young and believes region unappreciated	Early and adult self reliance		
		Lesser Adversaries		
		Early group experience; curiosity about region		
		Managerial experience; curiosity about region		

intervention as natural. Humanities or journalism majors, by contrast, are strongly against intervention. It is not immediately obvious why this contradiction should arise, but perhaps social science majors are associated with a substantive interest in the progress and problems of Latin America as a region. That interest may lead journalists to challenge government officials in the field. But it may also lead them to consider Latin America to be a "sphere of influence," the protection of which, from the perspective of the United States, may justify occasional intervention.

Perhaps the clearest preoccupational experience most strongly associated with professionalism, however, is a high level of educational achievement, specifically, earning a Master's degree. A Master's degree, although it appears to render journalists more tolerant of intervention, is nevertheless strongly and affirmatively associated with an examining perspective, and an adversarial posture in the field. Its absence is associated with a tolerance for East-West conflict. Holding a Master's credentials may represent a level of seriousness about journalism as a profession that is translated into high levels of professionalism for a variety of professional orientations.

News Organization Experience: Type of News Market and Career Path

Employer's Market

The visibility and size of market of a journalist's employer are significant, along with choice of a particular career path, in encouraging the learning of professional orientations. Although attitudes toward non-intervention and examining appear little affected by type of employer, professional attitudes toward an adversarial role and toward pluralism are associated with working outside a major wire-service news organization. This does not suggest that wire-service reporters are in any way less inherently capable of adversarial or pluralist reporting. Rather, the constraints placed on wire-service reporters by organizational necessity — both to file a large number of stories each day and to dispatch material suitable for markets throughout the world — diminish the amount of time necessary to think about a journalism encouraging elaborate professional possibilities. For this reason, perhaps, journalists who have worked for many years in the field in situations requiring a great deal of supervision or editing work are less likely to develop the professional perspectives examined in this study.

An observation by an experienced, distinguished reporter who worked for many years with the Associated Press will illustrate how important a particular kind of news organization is in placing boundaries on thought and action. In his book, *Coups and Earthquakes,* Mort Rosenblum notes that:

> The way a correspondent works depends on his medium. Reporters for news agencies, the pack horses of the profession, are by far the most harried. They are responsible for all news from their area, around the clock, seven days a week, and they are expected to report it faster than their competition. Virtually every daily newspaper, broadcast station, network and newsmagazine in the United States receives full time news wires of Associated Press, United Press International, or both. Most have no other source of foreign news. Those that do can always use AP or UPI when they wish. News agency reporters are squeezed from all sides. . . . When a major story breaks (he) must cover every aspect of it . . . because he is writing for newspapers around the world, there is no specific deadline. He must write a news story — or at least a new beginning — with every development.

> Since other types of correspondents have access to agency material, they can spend their time tracking down the junta leader or the guy who saved the triplets. Few of these correspondents share their best material with agency reporters because that might mean giving it to their competition. So after all the leg-work is done, agency reporters must then scramble to catch up with their colleagues' exclusives. (Rosenblum, 1979:27–28).

Career Path

In addition to the kind of organization a journalist works for, a reporter makes an important choice in pursuing a particular career path. Those who tend to move upward within a management framework, acquiring positions where they supervise more and more employees, and who are responsible for more organizational as opposed to reporting responsibilities, are likely to acquire one set of perspectives. Reporters who pursue a career path in which they continue as autonomous journalists, writing individually researched stories, are likely to consider themselves "solo craftsmen" and are likely to acquire a different set of attitudes.

In general, those who pursue careers as solo craftsmen, as individual reporters continuing to write their own material, are likely to be rather professional. Those who are solo craftsmen are most likely to be examining, to oppose intervention, and to be adversarial in the nation's capital. (The major exception to the observed link between solo craftsmanship and being professional is the finding that "solo craftsmen" are among the least adversarial in the field.)

In a complementary fashion, those who seem to describe themselves differently, as members of a team (not as individual performers), as experienced, and as lacking a Master's degree, are not likely to favor East-West pluralism. Experienced team players are less likely to be concerned about detente. Perhaps the tradition of the lone reporter and the self-reliant individual who is able to maintain his credibility and trust because he owes so little to others is a proud tradition in journalism. The data generated by this study suggest that the solo-craftsman tradition is a bulwark of professionalism among today's correspondents.

Friendship Experience

Friendship networks are associated with something contrary to expectation. Two kinds of friendship networks are examined in this study: friendships with nationals in the region or country of assignment and friendships with other journalists.

It might be assumed that friendship with nationals is associated with professional reporting perspectives because friendship represents a special level of concern and interest in a region and its people. The findings of this survey suggest, nevertheless, that having many Latin friends is associated positively only with being an adversary in the nation's capital. By contrast, having many Latin friends is curiously associated with little support for an examining perspective, non-intervention, and pluralism in East-West relations. Having enjoyed many Latin American friends also appears to have little relationship at all to a final measure of professionalism: demonstrating an adversarial perspective in the field, when reporting from Latin America. Friendship with nationals of a host country, therefore, is curiously associated with the formation not of professional but of non-professional perspectives as they are defined in this study.

In a similar fashion, the strength of friendship networks journalists form with other reporters exlains little about their professional perspectives. In their national survey of United States reporters, Johnstone, *et al.*, conclude that journalists who have a great many friendships with other journalists are likely to be what Johnstone and colleagues call "participatory," similar to what this survey calls "examining." But what Johnstone, *et al.*, found for reporters generally is not confirmed for the foreign correspondents surveyed in this study. Whether one has few or many friendships with other journalists has little to do with professional orientation, with one unusual exception. One type of journalist who is adversarial toward officials in the field has many journalist friends, while another type who is not adversarial in the field also had many journalist friends. In most cases, however, there is little or no relationship between friendship networks with other journalists and professional perspectives on reporting.

Findings Contrary to Expectation

The preceding discussion regarding friendship networks and professional perspectives reveals two sets of findings that are contrary to prevailing wisdom. Among correspondents who report on Latin America, those with relatively few friendships among host country nationals and those with some distance from their own colleagues are quite likely to display a variety of professional perspectives. Both conclusions contradict commonsense assumptions that reporters who know more about a region, develop friendships with nationals, and who are presumed to care more about a people of a region are likely to write material about that region in a professional manner along with journalists who interact frequently with their colleagues. Other conclusions can be drawn from the survey which are equally surprising.

Age and Generational Factors are Not Clearly Related to Professional Reporting perspectives

This analysis reveals that age plays a variety of roles in its impact on professional perspectives. Older and younger reporters (under forty-one or over fifty) are found among those who are adversarial in the nation's capital and among pluralists worried about East-West conflict. In addition, one type of reporter least likely to be an examiner is either younger or older (not in his forties). Further, age appears to have no relation at all to whether a journalist is for or against an adversarial orientation in the field. One type of journalist who tolerates intervention is in his forties, but considering all the findings, the evidence linking age to professional orientation is quite mixed. To the extent any conclusion is valid regarding age, it is that those in their forties are associated to some extent with opposition to two professional perspectives: examining and opposing intervention.

Finding that professionals — adversaries, pluralists, and even examiners — can be observed among younger and older correspondents is a significant empirical observation. It suggests that the development of the professional perspectives explored in this study is not simply the result of a "new generation" of reporters entering the field of reporting on foreign affairs. Learning to be a professional may be linked to something far more profound than a simple repetitive conflict or the emergence of a "generational shift." Rather, although rooted in events prior to the sixties, the appearance of professional perspectives is associated not simply with new people in journalism, but more profoundly with the development of a "critical" or "adversarial" culture.

To urge that a cultural shift has occurred suggests that what has happened in journalism transcends questions about "hostile" attitudes toward government or accusations leveled at a "small willful group of leftists." It not only agrees that a questioning perspective toward foreign affairs arose visibly in the late sixties and is to be found among young people both inside journalism and government, but also suggests that this perspective acquired the strength of a "cultural shift" and gathered the support of older journalists as well. Michael Schudson has explained this phenomenon in *Discovering the News: A Social History of American Newspapers:*

> The rebellion of young reporters in the sixties, then, was no mere repetition of perennial generational conflict in journalism; it was one manifestation of a social and cultural movement. The movement affected younger journalists first and most profoundly, but this, in turn influenced older and more powerful journalists. (Schudson, 1978:181).

Professional perspectives are therefore not the exclusive property of the young. Consistent with that observation is the finding that salary has little relation to professional perspectives as well. A good or at least middle-range salary, between $27,000 and $37,000 annually, is associated with one type of reporter who tolerates intervention. But neither age nor salary is a clear indicator that someone is likely to hold professional perspectives on foreign-affairs reporting.

Considerable Field Experience and Many Years Worked in Reporting on Latin America are Associated Primarily with a Negative Orientation Toward Professional Journalism

Total years of experience as a reporter is clearly related only to a low likelihood that a reporter is an examiner. Otherwise, total number of years worked as a journalist has little relation to the development of professional perspectives. Experience in regional or Latin American reporting, however, is related to the development of professional perspectives, but negatively so.

Although journalists with many years of experience writing about Latin America are likely to be adversarial toward officials in the field, they are less likely to acquire a pluralist perspective, or to oppose intervention, than are those with less experience reporting on the region. Furthermore, the amount of regional experience bears no relation to whether or not a reporter is likely to challenge officials in Washington, D.C. In general, the amount of regional experience a reporter gains in reporting on Latin America is either irrelevant in understanding the development of professional perspectives, or, if germane, is as likely to be associated with non-professional perspectives as with professional ones.

The Types of Sources Journalists Prefer Have Little Impact on Their Professional Perspectives

The factor analysis performed to yield an array of different types of reporters likely to learn professional perspectives reveals something unexpected. The sources preferred by different reporters — whether foreigners, local government officials, or nationals who are not government officials — appear to have relatively little influence on the acquisition of professional perspectives. The choice of source is made at a time when the reporter is actually in the field, engaged in reporting on a regular basis, or in a crisis. The choices among types of sources, however, are typically made before reporters have acquired a considerable amount of preoccupational and occupational experience.

The analysis described in this study reveals that these prior experiences have greater influence on reporter perspectives toward professional reporting than do more immediate choices about sources. Indeed, a reporter's ranking of preferred sources may sometimes be difficult to categorize in a suitably subtle fashion for each reporter and may be difficult to reduce to the maxims of social science. As one experienced journalist put it: "The task of reporting abroad is so complex that any correspondent asked the standard cocktail party question, 'Where do you get your news?,' invariably turns slightly greenish and edges towards the bar. It is like asking as waiter to recite a twelve page dinner menu." (Rosenblum, 1979:35).

An Overview Of Professional Correspondence

Several observations summarize the general conclusions derived from this multi-generational study of foreign correspondents who at some point in their lives have reported on Latin America.

There is More Than One Path to Professional Foreign Affairs Reporting

David Halberstam gained a great deal of notoriety for his role in challenging U.S. government perspectives on the war in Vietnam. Since he was employed at the time by *The New York Times,* a highly visible, prestigious newspaper, and was the occasion at least once of a critical comment by then-President John F. Kennedy, it might be assumed that adversaries in the David Halberstam tradition can flourish only at highly visible organizations that target the news to a select readership. The role of *The New York Times* as an institution has been enormously significant in serving as a "watchdog" on abuses in power, especially in publishing the Pentagon Papers; and institutional support doubtless played a significant and important role in maintaining Halberstam in his assignment in Vietnam, despite government concern. Professional foreign affairs reporters are nevertheless to be found not merely in select-market organizations, but also in news organizations that sell the news to a broad market.

For example, when David Halberstam was awarded a Pulitzer Prize for reporting the overthrow of South Vietnam's president Ngo Dinh Diem in November 1963, he shared that award with Malcolm Browne of the Associated Press (subsequently employed by the *Times*). Some believe that, had he not been out of the country in Tokyo at the time, Neil Sheehan, UPI's distinguished Saigon correspondent, would have shared the Pulitzer award. He was also subsequently employed by *The New York Times*. This suggests that whatever their institutional affiliations, the personal perspectives of individual journalists may play a critical role in transmitting professional reporting to the U.S. public.

Consistent with that example from Vietnam, this survey of reporters suggests there are many routes to the acquisition of a professional perspective on foreign-affairs journalism. Some examiners are solo craftsmen, others are group workers. Many of those with professional perspectives may lack regional expertise reporting on Latin America, but those reporters most likely to challenge officials in the field tend to be those with a great deal of regional expertise. Yet well-educated novices with many journalist friends also tend to be field adversaries, displaying little special regional experience.

A Number of the Champions of Professional Journalism May be Unheralded and Invisible

Despite the visibility of Pulitzer winners, professional reporters may be found in a variety of places and may not necessarily work for *The New York Times*. It is striking in this analysis that the clearest type of examiner is identified only as a full-time reporter with many siblings. This kind of professional is scattered throughout different news organizations and otherwise exhibits no consistent salary, age, or experience pattern. This inconspicuous reporter may presumably become more visible in crisis situations. Similarly, the type of reporter who most favors non-intervention doesn't necessarily work for any particular news organization, although he does tend to major in humanities or journalism, have several years military experience, and no Master's degree. In addition, the two kinds of reporters who are adversaries in the field are not found predominately to work for either select market or large market organizations. They are found throughout all types of organizations.

The Characteristics of Journalists Who are Opposed to, or Who Ignore, Modern Professional Perspectives Are More Coherent Than Those Who Favor Modern Professional Perspectives

There are many roads to the acquisition of modern professional reporting orientations, but there may be a relatively clear, single road away from learning to admire them. Two examples will suffice. Those who tend not to be examiners have spent many years as journalists, work in a team context, and lack Master's degrees. In similar fashion, those who tend not to be pluralists in favor of detente have spent many years reporting on Latin America, work in a team context, and lack Master's degrees. If a composite portrait were drawn of the kind of reporter least likely to be professional, it might be, curiously, the "good soldier," the stable, experienced reporter with many years of reporting on Latin America to his credit. By contrast, the types of reporters most likely to be highly professional are quite diverse in their background and experience, although self-reliance and "solo craftsman" orientations predominate.

A Considerable Amount of Learning is Transferred From Specific Family, Occupational, and Friendship Contexts to Professional Reporting Perspectives — Much of That Learning is Linked to Specific Choices Made by Individual Reporters

This analysis confirms that what reporters experience and learn prior to confronting crises is likely to provide coherent perspectives on reporting under crisis conditions. For example, responsibilities acquired early in a reporter's personal life may transfer to perspectives on an adversarial posture examining and East-West pluralism. Birth order affects one type of capital adversary, while sibling number influences becoming an examiner or pluralist.

Although journalists may not be able to select their birth order or sibling number, they do make clear educational choices about college major and whether to pursue a Master's degree. They also make clear career path choices early in their occupational histories, deciding whether to concentrate their energies on becoming "organization" types, moving up the editing and management hierarchy, or on becoming "solo craftsmen," striving for excellence as writers and news gatherers. A reporter's choice of employer may be less amenable to individual control than his choice of career path, given restricted employment opportunities for foreign correspondents. But since this study's findings reveal that foreign affairs reporters tend to work at a single news organization for many years, decisions about one's employer, especially about employer's market size (whether selective or broad), tend to be made early in a journalist's career.

As with educational and career path choices, specific friendship choices and the patterns they form can affect professional perspective on reporting. Whether to pursue friendships with nationals in the region of assignment, in this case Latin America, appears to exert a considerable impact on deeply held professional-reporting perspectives. And whether to include many or few fellow journalists among one's close friends affects the tendency of reporters to be adversarial toward officials in the field. In sum, specific experiences and decisions, often decisions concretized rather early in an individual's life-cycle, exert a profound impact on the very professional perspectives likely to prove most significant when a crisis occurs.

Strong Interest in the Region of Assignment, in This Case Latin America, is Seldom Associated with Professional Perspectives on Foreign Affairs Reporting

With the exception of adversaries (those who challenge officials either in the field or in Washington, D.C.), curiosity about the region of assignment (interest in the language, experience in reporting from the region, and friendships with nationals) is not associated with the acquisition of professional journalism perspectives. Those most likely to be examiners and both types of pluralists — those who favor non-intervention and those who favor detente — are likely to have acquired those reporting perspectives without the benefit of considerable curiosity about Latin America as a region or about its people. This conclusion suggests that to develop a professional perspective on foreign reporting, it is not always necessary to know a great deal about the region of assignment. It is important, however, to have learned coherent perspectives on the appropriate roles of reporters who have professional aspirations.

The Qualities that Encourage a Reporter to Be Adversarial in the "Field" Are Not Necessarily the Same Qualities that Promote an Adversarial Posture Inside the United States, Specifically in Washington, D.C.

Field and capital adversaries are similar in that they both display a genuine concern for the region of assignment, in this case Latin America. But differences between the two types of adversaries appear more prominent than similarities.

Field adversaries tend to exhibit considerable experience in reporting on

Latin America and appear to identify with journalism as at least a craft, and perhaps a profession. Many earn Master's degrees in journalism and claim many fellow journalists as friends. Capital adversaries, by contrast, are characterized primarily by a solo-craft orientation, supervising few people and displaying little field managerial experience and little team work experience. The "solo" quality of the capital adversary's professional orientation is rooted in experiences in early self-reliance: one type of capital adversary tends to be first-born. Continuity is apparent between early self-reliance and adult "lone reporter" perspectives.

In addition, capital adversaries often work for a particular news organization, a select-market daily paper or weekly magazine. They are less often found working for wire services. Overall, the qualities that define a field adversary are relatively diffuse, arrived at through age and experience writing about the region, whereas the qualities defining a capital adversary are relatively specific and coherent: a solo craftsman working for a specific type of employer whose adult perspectives are consistent with early sibling experience.

Professional Reporting Perspectives Are Linked Together

A number of different patterns can be identified as enduring throughout the variety of experiences encountered by foreign-affairs reporters. Those patterns include the following:

Professional perspectives may be acquired relatively early in a reporter's life or career.

There is more than one learning path to professional foreign affairs reporting.

At several points in the life-cycle, especially in its early phases, journalists may encounter serious choices with professional reverberations.

Some professional journalists can be found scattered throughout different types of news organizations.

The characteristics of journalists who are opposed to, or who ignore, modern professional perspectives are more coherent than those who favor modern professional perspectives.

Being an "adversary" toward government officials is not inherent in any particular journalistic "type," but rather varies with experience and reporting context.

Strong interest in the region of assignment, in this case Latin America, is seldom associated with professional perspectives on foreign affairs reporting.

TABLE 52   East-West Pluralism, Examining, and Non-Intervention

		Detente (East-West Pluralism)		
		Low %	Medium %	High %
Examining	High or Medium	46	68	74
	Low	54	32	26
		(37)	(22)	(34)

prob = .002

		Detente (East-West Pluralism)		
		Low %	Medium %	High %
Non-Inter-vention	High or Medium	31	52	66
	Low	69	48	34
		(35)	(21)	(35)

prob = .05

		Examining		
		Low %	Medium %	High %
Non-Inter-vention	High or Medium	86	68	75
	Low	14	32	25
		(36)	(34)	(20)

prob = .19

Multiple learning pathways apart, professional foreign affairs reporters are likely to acquire perspectives that are strongly related to one another and which form two clusters:

Adversaries
The two types of adversary orientations, field and capital, are closely linked. Those who are capital adversaries are also highly likely to be field adversaries as well. (This association is so strong it could occur by chance only 3 out of 1,000 times. Expressed differently, the association is significant at the .003 level.)

Pluralists, Examiners, and Non-Interventionists
A separate cluster, little related to an adversarial perspective, is also apparent. East-West pluralists are highly likely to be examiners (.002 level of

significance) and also non-interventionists (.05 level of significance). Examination of and opposition to intervention are also somewhat related (.19 level of significance), but the best predictor of both examination of and opposition to intervention is a pluralist orientation toward East-West conflict (see Table 52).

Two clusters of professional perspectives therefore emerge. One is adversarial. The other, if it can be referred to by the factor exerting the strongest amount of influence in its impact on other factors, is pluralist. These two professional orientations, adversarial and pluralist, are held by different types of journalists who have undergone correspondingly different learning experiences.

8

Professional Choices and Directions

A Search for New Conceptual Tools

Reporters form enduring perspectives that help them maintain their identities as journalists through the multiple demands confronting them. To identify these relatively fixed perspectives toward reporting as a profession, toward officials, and toward East-West issues is to suggest that internalized orientations can be considered useful tools in predicting what journalists are likely to do. New explanatory instruments are needed because the traditional ones available to journalists and scholars alike have proven inadequate.

Traditional views of reporting on the Third World appear to fall generally into two opposing camps. One view, which might be called an "individual perspective," focuses on personal and social differences among reporters and suggests that such differences account for diverse reporting outcomes. (Waugh, 1937; Gramling, 1940; Cooper, 1942; Hohenberg, 1964.) This perspective envisions enormous variation in individual attitudes, articles, and newspapers, and recognizes few reporting "patterns" among journalists or newspapers over time.

A second explanatory cluster may be considered to be the antithesis of the first and might be broadly called a "cultural" perspective. Focusing on sweeping cultural differences between the industrial world and the developing world, and on similarities among reporting from industrial countries, the "cultural" perspective draws attention to journalists as reflectors of broad cultural or information systems. (Galtung and Ruge, 1965; Elliott and Golding, 1973; Schiller, 1973; Mattleart, 1974; Beltrán, 1975; G.V. Robinson and V.M. Sparkes, 1976; Lent, 1977; Gerbner and Marvanyi, 1977; Rosengren, 1977.) Where the "individual" perspective might view the industrial world, and U.S. reporters in particular, as atomized and disparate, the cultural viewpoint sees them as engaged in generally similar reporting.

Much of this cultural literature is insightful in describing several "regularities" in foreign news channels, "regularities" reflecting perhaps conventional reporting "codes" and/or "routines" of news gathering. Galtung and Ruge (1965) have ably described Swedish perspectives on news from the Third World, and Elliott and Golding (1973) have assembled a similar list of "regularities" in British coverage of foreign affairs. News-gathering regularities linked to a North American perspective on the world have been recently described by Herbert Gans in *Deciding What's News* (1978). He lists the following themes as commonly found in U.S. reporting of events abroad:

1. American activities in a foreign country;
2. Foreign activities that affect Americans and American policy;
3. Communist-bloc country activities; a) activities perceived to involve their relationship to the United States; and b) internal problems or difficulties that reduce their military, economic, or political power vis-a-vis the United States. (Gans suggests that "almost everything that happens in a Communist-bloc country is thought to affect Americans or American policy, which helps explain why so much of the foreign news comes from countries within that bloc." (Gans, 1978:33);
4. Elections and other changes in government personnel;
5. Political conflict and protest;
6. Disasters; and
7. The excesses of dictatorship. (Gans, 1978: 31–37).

While some authors have examined cultural, economic and political continuities and regularities in industrial-world reporting on the Third World, other scholars focus specifically on U.S. reporting about Latin America. Al Hester finds considerable emphasis on violence in U.S. reporting on Latin America. (Hester, 1974: 82–98.) Jerry Knudson has concluded that U.S. reporting is far more critical of social change when political and social change come from the left than when they come from the right. (Knudson, 1974a, 1974b, 1974c, 1978.) John Lent has drawn attention to national interest as a factor affecting U.S. reporting on countries to the south (Lent, 1977: 46–51), and John Crothers Pollock and Christopher Guidette have drawn attention to national strategic interests as an important aspect of U.S. coverage of Latin America and South Africa. (Pollock and Guidette, 1980.) Such studies document specific cultural, political, and economic perspectives in coverage of a particular region in the Third World: Latin America.

In an effort to make predictions about the direction and content of foreign affairs reporting, the "cultural" approach is often preferable to the "individual" one. The "individual" perspective sees each reporter or news institution as rather unique and suggests that these unique, individual differences are retained when reporting on events abroad. The "cultural" perspective, by contrast, searches for patterns in reporting on foreign affairs, and in doing so, makes possible the construction of hypothetical predictive guesses about the way industrial countries report on the Third World over long periods of time. As an analytical and predictive tool, the "cultural" perspective, which often relies on content analysis of distinct newspapers for evidence, is a useful device. An important limit must nevertheless be recognized. The literature on cultural or news channel "regularities" is used most appropriately to predict precisely that: regularities. Crises are by definition "irregular" events, and coverage of crises may not be amenable to explanations used to describe broad patterns over long periods of time. In order to make predictions about what reporters and news institutions are likely to do in crisis situations, a different analytical tool may be required.

This study has suggested that, in order to understand what may happen in a crisis, it is useful to examine the way journalists learn professional orientations on foreign-affairs reporting. Thus far, this analysis has identified several relevant perspectives and traced the learning pathways leading some journalists, rather than others, to acquire these professional orientations. Beyond the tasks of identifying professional perspectives and tracing their development, a serious question remains: "How do such perspectives affect crisis reporting?" That query is the concern of this chapter.

One way to begin answering questions about the impact of professional orientations on crisis journalism is to suggest a simple content analysis of crisis reporting, linking the professional orientations of individual reporters with the direction and content of articles attributed to such reporters. Such an approach might be useful over many crises and where many different crises and many different reporters are selected for examination, but it is an approach fraught with difficulty, because many factors may intervene between what a reporter believes and what his news organization prints.

Most correspondents surveyed in this study remain at one news institution for most of their careers and can be presumed to acquire or at least accommodate many of the news perspectives found at their own news organizations. It is nevertheless difficult to study systematically or account for the following questions:

1. How does a news organization decide to select some material from a wire-service source and some from its own correspondents?
2. How do editors decide to select some articles rather than others from a given correspondent for publication?

3. How do correspondent opinion and editorial and publisher judgment interact if they do so at all to produce a particular perspective on news from the field?

These and other questions dramatize the difficulty of establishing any direct relationship or one-to-one correspondence between the professional perspectives of foreign affairs journalists and what a news organization prints about a particular crisis.

This survey of foreign affairs journalists reporting on Latin America nevertheless does permit a scholarly assessment of three arenas of inquiry that measure how likely reporters are to make their professional perspectives heard or known under conditions of crisis. The three topics can be expressed as distinct questions:

1. What do broad learning patterns reveal about the flexibility of reporters under crisis conditions?
2. How likely are foreign affairs reporters to make known their views or what they consider the public's views to U.S. foreign policy officials under crisis conditions?
3. How likely are foreign affairs reporters to encourage the formation of a relatively strong professional organization — similar to those found in law or medicine — in order to form a more disciplined, potent organization for professional journalism?

One Learning Process Prevails

In tracing the possible learning patterns foreign affairs reporters are likely to experience, the second chapter of this study identifies three learning models as likely pathways. One is cumulative and gradual. The second is contained and rather rigid. The third is discontinuous and abrupt. The data gathered in this study suggest that for most foreign affairs reporters, learning professional journalism perspectives is a gradual, cumulative process. Some contained and discontinuous learning occur, but in most cases, gradual learning describes the socialization process journalists undergo.

The Importance of Prior Experience

In describing a learning or socialization approach to the study of foreign affairs journalists, Chapter Two suggests that both prior experience and immediate social context might each have a significant impact on the professional perspectives of reporters. This analysis of a survey of foreign affairs journalists reporting on Latin America, however, suggests that prior experience is far more important than immediate social context and that early learning about the world foreshadows and indeed foretells later learning. This survey reveals that early sibling experience is strongly related to later adult learning about professional perspectives toward journalism. Both birth order and total number of siblings has a capacity to affect his later views about reporting as a profession and about a topic of immense social and political significance: East-West conflict. Choices made while in college also have a significant impact on orientations held with conviction many years later. The choice of a discipline, either in the social sciences, the humanities, or journalism itself, has a clear bearing on attitudes held by adult journalists many years later, as does a decision whether or not to complete a Master's degree. Preoccupational experience, including both early sibling experience and educational choices in college, have a clear impact on journalist's views about professional reporting.

Other decisions made early in a journalist's career are also likely to contribute in important ways to professional perspectives on foreign affairs reporting. The news organization a journalist chooses to work for is likely to make a clear impression on professional development, especially if that decision involves a choice between a wire-service organization appealing to a broad market and a news organization that targets its news at a more select market. Most journalists work for many years for the same organization: 32 percent have worked more than eighteen years for the same organization and another 34 percent have worked between eleven and seventeen years for a single organization. Since foreign affairs reporters work for many years for the same organization, it is reasonable to conclude they make significant decisions early in their careers about which news organization they will seek as an employer. Choice of employer makes a measureable impact on professional orientations toward foreign affairs journalism, and it is a choice made often in the early stages of a successful journalist's career.

A reporter's choice of career path, whether as a solo craftsman or as a manager, may also be made relatively early in a journalism career. The perception of such a choice may not become immediately apparent to a young journalist, but will certainly become apparent as he becomes more experienced. In addition, a journalist's choice of friends and non-friends, especially regarding friendships among nationals of a host country, may make a dramatic contribution to deeply held attitudes toward professional reporting.

Each of the preceding experiences, with siblings, schooling, employer, and career path, is, or may be, undergone relatively early in a journalist's career. Some of the early experiences with schooling are consistent with choice of news organization and choice of career path. Finding major factors affecting the professional viewpoints of journalists at so many stages in a journalist's career confirms a major assumption of this study: early learning has a substantial impact on adult, in this case professional, attitudes and orientations toward reporting.

The evidence for multiple points of learning along an individual's life cycle also indicates that such learning is relatively gradual, rooted in an individual's past, with additions made incrementally as he grows to professional maturity. The evidence for the importance of early learning and its contribution to later learning reinforce the conclusion that the kinds of learning and experiences most relevant for professional reporting among mature journalists are essentially cumulative; few rigidities or abrupt discontinuities are apparent. Because this study documents the accuracy of accumulative learning path, an accumulative model may be used to describe the changes undergone by reporters who, through questions arising from the Bay of Pigs, the Dominican Republican intervention of 1965, the Tet Offensive of 1968 in Vietnam, the Pentagon Papers, and all of the other events that led so many to question so much about U.S. foreign policy, gradually reinterpreted views about that policy and about social change in the Third World.

Little Confirmation of Contained or Discontinuous Learning

Because this study reveals so clearly that journalists have undergone a gradual, incremental learning process, there is little evidence for the presence of contained or continuous learning. Two examples nevertheless demonstrate the appearance of those two other types of learning.

Contained learning is characterized by the congruence of later and early learning and with a learning process in which adult maturing simply reinforces what was learned early in life. One finding in the study provides evidence for a constrained learning trajectory. It has been discovered that a generation of foreign affairs journalists, in their forties, are least likely to be adversarial toward officials in Washington, D.C., and although those manifesting an examining perspective are generally younger, a high proportion of strong examiners are found among reporters over fifty. Journalists in their forties, by contrast, apparently consider themselves to be quite comfortable with officials and with official perspectives.

In the late 1940s and 1950s, those who are in their forties today were between the approximate ages of twenty and thirty, just beginning their careers. Confirming a major conclusion of the study, early career learning for one group of journalists in their forties has apparently remained relatively congruent with their perspectives on foreign affairs reporting today. A plausible reason for such reinforced learning is immediately apparent. Such journalists entered their careers during a period when East-West conflict was a prevailing maxim of strategic thought among officials in the United States government, the period of the late 1940s and 1950s. Since early learning may be formative, relatively permanent, and difficult to change, then it is not entirely unexpected that journalists who entered their careers in a period of substantial East-West conflict should have retained collegial perspectives toward officials with such tenacity into the present.

The same paucity of evidence for "contained" learning is found in the scarcity of data suggesting discontinued learning. It can be recalled that discontinuous learning involves a qualitative, or quantum, change in perspective, or a new orientation formed by an an abrupt rupture with previous viewpoints. It also involves a learning process involving what can be described as compartmentalization, or specification, isolating one kind of learning from a previous kind. Although there is little evidence that individual journalists in this study manifest discontinuities or experience abrupt ruptures from the past, there is evidence that news organizations may do so.

In comments made before the Columbia University's University Seminar on Public Communications, October 15, 1980, Harrison Salisbury, formerly of *The New York Times,* commented on his recent book, *Without Fear or Favor.* He described an abrupt shift in perspective which occurred in *The New York Times* regarding the war in Vietnam, documenting the concern demonstrated by executives of the *Times* for the continuous efforts of various secret government agencies to gain a foothold in *The New York Times.* He also described the abrupt shift that occurred in the newspaper when it, or rather Arthur Ochs "Punch" Sulzberger, decided to publish the Pentagon Papers. With the publication of those documents, *The New York Times,* according to Salisbury, changed its role from simply reporting, or in terms of this study, "chronicling" official pronouncements and activities, to a "monitoring" role, acting as a surrogate for the public interest, attempting to examine and bring public issues to light. Although Salisbury traced the roots of this shift in the previous foreign affairs reporting not simply of David Halberstam, but also of Robert Trumbull and Homer Bigart, the former *Times* executive also described the decision to publish the Pentagon Papers and to challenge the United States government as a major shift of perspective for one of the country's most prestigious newspapers.

Occasional examples apart, this study of reporters covering Latin America for major news institutions confirms the impression that a great deal of learning that affects professional-reporting perspectives is acquired relatively early in a reporter's life, and subsequent contacts and interactions are significant mainly to the extent they are consistent with that early learning. Since early learning is deeply embedded, and since later learning is primarily grafted onto that core of early learning experience, it can be expected that journalists described in this study acquire relatively early a serious set of coherent orientations toward reporting as a profession. Since such orientations have been initiated early and developed gradually, it is likely that they are maintained with considerable tenacity. It is also likely, therefore, that foreign affairs journalists may exhibit little flexibility in shifting such orientations under crisis conditions. The early acquisition of professional perspectives on foreign affairs journalism suggests that they have a profound impact on adult reporters and are likely to guide values and principles under crisis conditions.

Learning A Participatory Perspective

The professional-reporting orientations acquired by respondents appear rooted in their personal world views, but how likely are they to make those perspectives known under crisis conditions? One effort to assess that likelihood is made possible by testing how much reporters agree or disagree that journalists should bring public views and needs to the attention of State Department officers. This attitude dimension is a measure of professional "participation": it measures how likely reporters are to view their role not simply as transmitters and recipients of information, but rather as participants bringing significant information to the attention of policy makers.

Table 53 reveals the distribution of responses according to levels of agreement with the mentioned statement: "Reporters should bring public views and needs to the attention of State Department officers." Almost half (48 percent) disagree somewhat or disagree strongly; about one out of five (22 percent) neither agree or disagree; and only three out of ten agree strongly or somewhat with the statement and can be considered strongly participatory. Respondents likely to believe they can appropriately "participate" in foreign-policy decision-making by making public views known to State Department officials tend to exhibit many of the same characteristics and experiences displayed by examiners, adversaries, and pluralists (see Table 53).

Life-Cycle Factors

Reporter "participants" are relatively young. About two-thirds (66 percent) of those forty or under are participatory, compared to a little over four out of ten of those over forty. Consistent with other findings in this study concerning attitudes toward detente, about two thirds of the respondents (68 percent) who attended less prestigious schools favor participation, far more

TABLE 53   Participatory Perspective

	%		Collapsed %
Agree Strongly	10	Agree	28
Agree	18	Neither Agree or Disagree	21
Neither Agree nor Disagree	21	Disagree	45
Disagree	20		
Disagree Strongly	25		
	(94)		(94)

than those who attended more prestigious state universities or elite schools (44 percent). Further, seven out of ten who have Masters' degrees favor a participatory perspective, compared to only about half (52 percent) who hold only Bachelors' degrees. Finally, those still married to original spouses are relatively participatory. Finding that younger reporters, those from less prestigious schools, and those with Master's degrees favor a participatory perspective is consistent with other findings about professional perspectives in this study (see Table 54).

Organizational Factors

Organizational factors also predict participatory orientations that are consistent with other findings in the study. Those journalists who are engaged entirely in reporting (as opposed to managing) currently, who supervise few employees, who see themselves more as individual than as team players, and who do not work for a wire service are likely to be highly participatory.

About six out of ten journalists who devote most of their time purely to reporting activities are participatory, compared to only four out of ten who are engaged in other managerial activities. Consistent with the association between reporting and a participatory attitude, over half (57 percent) of those who supervise five or fewer employees are participatory, compared to

TABLE 54   Participation by Age, Degree Status, Educational Achievement, Marital Stability

| | Age | | | | B.A. Status | |
	40 or Less %	41–50 %	51 or More %		Other %	Elite or State University %
High or Medium	66	44	46	High or Medium	68	44
Low	34 (32)	56 (27)	54 (35)	Low	32 (40)	56 (41)
prob = .26				prob = .22		

| | Master's Degree | | | | Married to Original Spouse | |
	Yes %	No %			Yes %	No %
High or Medium	70	52	High or Medium		58	39
Low	30 (20)	48 (60)	Low		42 (66)	61 (28)
prob = .20				prob = .19		

only about four out of ten (38 percent) who supervise six or more employees. Also consistently, about three-fourths who believe themselves to function in their occupation primarily as individuals or to operate as individuals at least half the time are participatory, compared to only about one-third who believe they operate primarily in a team framework (see Table 55).

Finally, there is a clear relationship between working outside a wire service and holding a participatory perspective toward foreign-policy officials. Only about four out of ten of those who work for wire services (37 percent) are participatory compared to about two-thirds (65 percent) who work outside the wire services. A clear majority (61 percent) of those who have worked many years for major dailies other than *The New York Times* or the *Washington Post* (e.g., the *Los Angeles Times* and the *Miami Herald*) are participatory. Curiously, those who are somewhat disappointed in their own news organizations are also likely to be highly participatory. Among respondents who wish to work outside their own news organizations in the next five years, 42 percent are very participatory, compared to only 21 percent who hope to work for the same news organization (see Table 56).

Friendship Network Factors

In their life-cycle and organizational experiences, participatory respondents are similar to respondents who acquire other professional perspectives. An examination of their friendship networks, however, reveals some startling differences. Although they are currently solo craftsmen, most respondents who are participatory say that they did managerial work in Latin America, compared to less than half who engaged entirely in reporting work. Managerial status apart, they appear to have spent a great deal of time outside capital cities in Latin America with over five out of ten participants (54 percent) traveling a great deal outside capital cities, compared to only 38 percent who seldom traveled outside such cities.

The startling departure from other patterns, however, is that those who are participatory in informing foreign policy officials about public views and needs say they tend to have many friendships among Latin American nationals. About six out of ten (62 percent) who say their primary friendships in the field are not with other correspondents are participatory, compared to only four out of ten (41 percent) whose friends are other correspondents. Similarly, about two-thirds (64 percent) who say their best friends in the field are Latin American nationals are participatory, compared to only a little more than three out of ten (32 percent) who say their best friends in the field are not nationals of the host country. Finally, among those who interact most with foreign or local officials as sources, 56 percent are participatory, compared to only 35 percent who rely on non-officials.

TABLE 55 Participation by Supervisory Responsibility and Teamwork Context

| | Number of Employees Supervised | | Teamwork Context | |
	Five or Fewer %	Six or More %	Individual or Half Time %	Teamwork More Than 50% of Time %
Participation High or Medium	57	38	64	44
Low	43	62	36	56
	(70)	(24)	(28)	(62)

prob = .03   prob = .18

TABLE 56 Participation by Employing Organization and Preferred Future Position

	Employer		Employer Select Market			
	Wire Service %	Non-Wire Service %	Broad Market (Wire Service) %	(Major Dailies) %	(Major Weeklies) %	N.Y. Times Wash. Post %
Participation High or Medium	37	65	37	61	71	64
Low	63	35	63 (43)	39 (18)	29 (14)	36 (19)

prob = .006   prob = .002

Preferred Employment After Five Years

	Same Organization %	Elsewhere in Media or Outside Media %
Participation High	21	42
Medium or Low	79 (56)	58 (26)

prob = .04

In sum, those journalists likely to participate actively in bringing public views and needs to the attention of U.S. foreign-policy officials are relatively young and well-educated, solo craftsmen, and, strikingly, share friendships with nationals of the host countries in which they are posted (see Table 57).

Links with Other Professional Perspectives

Being a participant is connected somewhat with two other professional perspectives already discussed, being adversarial in Washington, D.C., and favoring detente. Sixty-eight percent of those who are capital adversaries are also participatory, compared to only 45 percent who are not capital adversaries. Similarly, among those who favor detente moderately, almost seven of ten (68 percent) are quite participatory. But the clearest link discovered is between being a participant and favoring a strong, authoritative, or professional journalism association, the topic of the next section (see Table 58).

Learning Disciplinary Perspectives

It is clear that the professional orientations of foreign affairs journalists are embedded in experiences undergone over the course of individual life cycles, and it is also clear that many of the same journalists who hold professional perspectives are willing to express their concerns and sensitivities regarding public opinion to official policy makers. It is less clear, however, whether foreign affairs journalists are likely to regard professional concerns so seriously that they're willing to strengthen the authority of a professional journalism organization.

To discover how willing foreign correspondents are to hold their colleagues to certain principles of professional practice, respondents were asked to rate a number of statements according to how much they agreed or disagreed with them. Each statement said something about professional standards of journalism. Using Guttman scaling procedures, four of the statements were found to be unidimensional and can be combined to form a single scale or factor, here called a disciplinary orientation. The four components of that scale are the following:

For the working journalists there should be required periodic institutes or refresher courses, e.g. in economics or political science (25 percent agree or agree completely);

If a member of a professional journalism organization commits an unprofessional action (e.g. takes a bribe), he should be disciplined by the professional organization, regardless whether or not formal legal action has been taken (48 percent agree or agree completely);

TABLE 57 Participation by Field Experience Outside Cities, Friendship Patterns, and Preferred Sources

	Annual Travel Outside Capital Cities		Field Friendship Network	
	2 Months or Less %	More Than 2 Months %	Other Correspondents %	Non-Correspondents %
Participation				
High or Medium	38	54	41	62
Low	62 (24)	46 (61)	59 (46)	38 (32)

prob = .10   prob = .04

	Best Friends in Field		Preferred Sources	
	Not Nationals %	Host Country National %	Foreign Sources Local Officials %	Local Non-Officials %
Participation				
High or Medium	35	32	64	56
Low	68 (37)	36 (45)	44 (45)	65 (26)

prob = .015   prcb = .10

TABLE 58   Participation by Capital Adversarial and Detente Orientation

| | | Capital Adversary | | Detente Orientation | | |
		Low %	High %	Low %	Medium %	High %
Participation	High or Medium	45	68	46	68	48
	Low	55	32	54	32	52
		(29)	(40)	(37)	(19)	(33)
prob = .12			prob = .13			

Professions such as law and medicine have developed organizations to up-
hold professional standards. Journalists themselves should form an
organization to deal with problems that come up and to supervise the
profession (50 percent agree completely, agree, agree somewhat, or only
disagree somewhat);
A journalist should be certified by his professional organization as to quali-
fications, training, and compétence (57 percent agree completely, agree,
agree somewhat, disagree somewhat, or disagree).[1]

The preceding statements and levels of agreement associated with them
demonstrate the extent to which journalists believe a professional journalist
organization should be given some authority to discipline its members. The
percentages listed after each statement, along with the ranges of agreement
indicated, reveal different levels of agreement journalists register for each
statement. Table 59 reveals the distribution of respondents according to their
levels of agreement or disagreement with the overall disciplinary orientation
scale. About 33 percent are highly disciplnary, 18 percent are moderately
disciplinary, and about half (48 percent) are relatively non-disciplinary in
their attitudes toward disciplined journalism.[2] This hardly suggests a
massive wave of a support for more professional discipline in journalism,
but it does suggest that a substantial number of correspondents regard professional journalism as a matter of serious concern. The following information suggests which types of reporters are most likely to favor a disciplinary
profession (see Table 59).

The reporters most likely to favor the formation of a disciplinary professional organization, similar to one found in the professions of law or
medicine, appear to exhibit quite specific traits. In their life cycle histories,
most disciplinarians are strongly vocational, tend to be more experienced
than those who wish less discipline, and demonstrate confined career patterns. Most of them did not work outside of journalism before becoming
journalists. Unlike others who favor professional orientations toward officials and toward pluralism, disciplinarians tend to be team players rather
than craftsmen. Also unlike others who demonstrate a concern for profes-

TABLE 59 Disciplinary Orientation

	%		Adjusted %
Most Disciplinary	14	High	33.3
Highly Disciplinary	19		
Somewhat Disciplinary	18	Medium	18.3
Little Disciplinary	27		
Least Disciplinary	22	Low	48.4
	(93)		(93)

sionalism in foreign affairs reporting, many disciplinarians appear to be dissatisfied with their work in their employing news organizations. In addition, disciplinarians tend to work for wire-service employers.

Although organizational factors predominate, at least two friendship-network factors are associated with a disciplinary perspective. Those who report having some government friends who are officials are more likely to accept the notion of discipline and professional rules. In addition, a very strong association is found between those who have many Latin American friends and a preference for professional discipline. Specific findings follow.

Life-cycle Factors

Being first-born, majoring in journalism, and not completing a Master's degree are all associated with a disciplinary perspective. About six out of ten who are first-born are disciplinary, compared to only about four out of ten (43 percent) born later in their families. Early self-reliance predicts adult concern for standardized professional norms and values.

A tendency to study directly vocational topics is also linked to a disciplinary perspective, along with least-privileged schooling. Seven out of ten journalism majors are disciplinary, compared to only about five out of ten humanities majors and four out of ten social-science majors. Consistent with a vocationalist perspective, only about 45 percent of those with time-consuming Master's degrees are disciplinary, compared to 60 percent of those who have only earned a Bachelor's degree. Vocationalism apart, non-privileged schooling is also associated with a disciplinary perspective. Among those who attended elite colleges and universities, only 43 percent are disciplinarians, compared to 58 percent from state universities and about two-thirds (66 percent) from less renowned colleges (see Table 60).

Organizational Factors

Disciplinarians tend to be team players rather than solo craftsmen. Those who have less than total reporting responsibilities (perhaps editing on managing as well), and who feel part of a team effort, are likely to want a

TABLE 60 Disciplinary Perspective by Birth Order, College Major, Educational Achievement, and College Status

		Birth Order		College Major		
		Later Born %	First Born %	Social Sciences %	Humanities %	Journalism %
Disciplinary	High or Medium	43	61	40	53	71
	Low	57 (47)	39 (46)	60 (20)	47 (32)	29 (24)

		Master's Degree		Other %	College Status Elite or State University %
		Yes %	No %		
Disciplinary	High or Medium	45	60	66	48
	Low	55 (22)	40 (57)	34 (38)	52 (42)

prob = .50

prob = .27

strong professional organization. Between five and six out of ten who spend less than two-thirds of their time reporting are disciplinary, compared to about four out of ten (37 percent) who engage in reporting essentially all the time. Almost six out of ten (57 percent) who believe they work in a team framework at least 50 percent of the time are disciplinary, compared to about one-third (36 percent) who believe they work mostly as individuals (see Table 61).

Those with special kinds of reporting histories are more likely to be disciplinarian than others. About six out of ten respondents (58 percent) who began reporting on Latin America prior to 1957 are likely to be disciplinary, compared to only about 50 percent of those who began reporting on Latin America more recently. The more experience one has in reporting on Latin America, the more disciplinary one is likely to be. Similarly, those who began their careers immediately in journalism without trying other kinds of careers are also likely to be disciplinary. Fifty-seven percent of those who have devoted their entire careers to journalism are disciplinary, compared to only 33 percent of those who have tried other careers prior to becoming reporters. Those with considerable experience in reporting on Latin America and those who have dedicated themselves entirely to reporting as a vocational pursuit are likely to take professional disciplinary measures quite seriously and to believe they have merit. Despite their long experience in journalism, disciplinarians earn rather low salaries (below $27,500). Almost two-thirds (63 percent) of those with salaries below this amount are disciplinarians, compared to less than half of those who earn higher annual salaries (see Table 62).

It is curious, given this history of solid accomplishment as dedicated reporters experienced in regional matters, that those journalists least satisfied with the organizations employing them are most likely to favor a disciplinary profession. About six out of ten (62 percent) who prefer to work in some other organization or outside of media in the next five years are disciplinary compared to only about four out of ten (45 percent) who said they would like to remain in the same organization during the next five years. Perhaps those who believe their dedication and experience have been little appreciated, or that their personal standards have received little recognition within their organizations, are likely to look outside such organizations to professional associations for support. Or perhaps some journalists believe that, regardless of their own experiences, the maintenance of professional standards cannot be left to the judgment or jurisdiction of any single news organization (see Table 63).

Teamwork, long experience, and disappointment apart, journalists working for a broad news-market organization are most likely to favor a disciplinary professional association. Six out of ten who work for wire services are disciplinary, compared to about 50 percent of those who work for

TABLE 61　Disciplinary Perspective by Current Reporting Responsibilities and Teamwork Context

| | | Percent Time Spent on Reporting Responsibilities | | | Teamwork Context | |
		None %	Up to 65% %	66% or More %	Individual %	Teamwork 50 Percent of Time or More %
Disciplinary	High or Medium	53	62	37	36	57
	Low	47	38	63	64	43
		(36)	(26)	(27)	(28)	(62)
prob = .21				prob = .14		

166

TABLE 62 Disciplinary Perspective by Years of Regional and Journalism Reporting Experience, and Salary Level

| | | Year Began Reporting on Latin America | | | Other Careers Prior to Journalism | |
		Pre-Sputnik %	Post Sputnik Pre-Tet %	Post-Tet %	Yes %	No %
Disciplinary	High or Medium	58	49	50	57	33
	Low	42 (24)	51 (37)	50 (30)	43 (72)	67 (21)

prob = .56   prob = .15

| | | Salary Level (In Dollars) | | |
		$27,499 or Less %	$27,500–37,499 %	$37,500 or More %
Disciplinary	High or Medium	63	49	44
	Low	37 (30)	51 (35)	56 (27)

prob = .39

TABLE 63   Disciplinary Perspective by Preferred Employment After Five Years

| | Preferred Employment After Five Years | |
	In Same Organization %	Elsewhere Inside or Outside Media %
High or Medium	45	62
Low	55	38
	(55)	(26)

prob = .18

major news weeklies and the major dailies reporting on Latin America other than *The New York Times* or the *Washington Post*. Only four out of ten who work for the last two dailies mentioned are likely to be disciplinary. This information suggests that working at the wire services, with their large markets and vast complex organizational structure, is associated with holding clear disciplinary perspectives. Working for the *Washington Post* or *The New York Times,* by contrast, much smaller organizations permitting more autonomy, is associated with less attention paid to professional disciplinary measures.

Network Factors

Organizational experience is the major factor predicting disciplinary perspectives. Only two friendship factors are clearly associated with the preference for discipline in a journalist's professional association. The first is that about six out of ten (62 percent) of those who report that over 10 percent of their off-duty friends are government officials are likely to support the concept of a disciplinary professional association for journalists, compared to only five out of ten (51 percent) who say they have few or no official friends. This finding suggests that those who are accustomed to discussions of rule-making, enforcement, and rule adjudication for society in general may also be comfortable with discussions of rule arrangements for their own professional associations.

The second friendship factor associated with a disciplinary perspective is even more powerful than the first. Other sections of this study have noted that those who have very few Latin American friends are likely to be quite professional in their preference for an examining reporting posture, an adversarial stance toward officials, and a pluralist perspective on international affairs. In this instance, however, those who say their best friends when in Latin America are Latin Americans are by far the strongest supporters of a disciplinary professional association. Almost six out of ten (61 percent) of the respondents who report their best friends are from Latin America are disciplinary, compared to only about four out of ten (38 percent) respondents who say their best friends, when stationed in Latin America, are from the United States. Both friendships with officials and friendships with citizens of Latin America, consistent with a large amount of experience in reporting on the region, are clearly associated with a willingness to view disciplinary measures as useful for the vitality of a professional journalism association (see Table 64).

A Disciplinary Perspective and Other Professional Orientations

Those who favor a strong, authoritative professional association are not likely to be examiners, but they do tend to be participants, drawing official attention to personal and public views. Table 65 illustrates these two relationships. Since there is a negative relation between disciplinary and examining perspectives, it is clear that examining's opposite, a chronicler perspective, is clearly linked to a wish for stronger authority in professional associations. Those who value examining highly may not wish to relinquish their personal opportunities in exchange for strong professional standards (see Table 65).

In general, those respondents least likely to hold professional perspectives favoring examining, an adversarial stance toward officials, or East-West pluralism are strikingly the very journalists most likely to favor a strong, disciplinary professional journalism organization. Those journalists willing to look favorably at a more centralized journalism profession tend to display specific life-cycle, organizational, and social network experiences: They exhibit early vocational tendencies, majoring in journalism and choosing not to pursue an advanced degree. They usually have some editing or managing responsibilities and regard themselves not as solo craftsmen but as part of a team effort. They tend to work for wire services and rarely for *The New York Times* or the *Washington Post*. Although they are among the most experienced reporters, their salaries are curiously among the lowest, and they tend to be somewhat disappointed with journalism. Most of the respondents who believe they would like to work outside of journalism in the next five years are disciplinary, compared to a majority of disciplinarians who would like to remain in journalism. Disciplinarians do not resemble other professionals.

TABLE 64   Disciplinary Perspective by Employing Organization, and Friendship Patterns

		Employer		Broad Market	Employer Select Market		
		Wire Service %	Non-Wire Service %	(Wire Service) %	(Major Dailies) %	(Major Weeklies) %	(N.Y. Times or Post) %
Disciplinary	High or Medium	60	45	60	50	47	40
	Low	40 (40)	55 (53)	40 (40)	50 (16)	53 (17)	60 (20)

prob = .36   prob = .76

		Off Duty Friendships with Government Employees		Best Friends in the Field	
		Some (Over 10%) %	Few or More %	Not Nationals %	Host Country Nationals %
Disciplinary	High or Medium	65	46	38	61
	Medium	35 (23)	54 (70)	62 (37)	39 (44)

prob = .08

*Probability is unknown

TABLE 65   Disciplinary Perspective by Examining and Participation

		Examining			Participation		
		Low %	Medium %	High %	Low %	Medium %	High %
Disciplinary	High or Medium	53	58	37	42	40	76
	Low	47	42	63	58	60	24
		(32)	(38)	(19)	(41)	(20)	(25)
prob. = .18					prob. = .03		

Predicting The Future

The preceding observations confirm the expectation that the professional orientations of foreign-affairs reporters have a significant bearing on the likelihood that they will find those perspectives appropriate under conditions of ambiguity or crisis. In such situations, deeply held perspectives may combine with a willingness to communicate individual perceptions to officials. Among some reporters who are least likely to hold the professional perspectives discussed in this study, there is a readiness to welcome outside help from a strong professional journalists' association in monitoring the conduct of reporters. These conclusions, together with observations derived from the preceding chapters, permit the construction of several predictions for the immediate future.

U.S. Journalists are Not a Monolithic, Homogeneous Group

In international information debates, it is sometimes charged that industrial-world reporters share markedly similar assumptions and viewpoints in their perspectives on events in the Third World. From inside the industrial world, a number of differences in reporting on Third World crises are apparent, even between the two major English-speaking countries, Great Britain and the United States. (Hart, 1966; Pollock and Guidette, 1980). This survey of foreign-affairs reporters covering Latin America for major U.S. news organizations finds further differences among U.S. reporters in their attitudes toward the reporting profession, toward officials, and toward East-West strategic policy. Examining each of these dimensions, some reporters are more professional than others.

A Small Number of Factors Derived from the Preoccupational and Occupational Experiences of Foreign-Affairs Journalists Exert a Vast Influence on Their Professional Perspectives on Reporting

Although the reporters surveyed in this study are far from homogeneous, the variation in their responses is not infinite. Their responses fall into a number of relatively clear patterns. A very small number of factors account for those patterns, specifically: birth order and number of siblings, educational focus (college major) and level of achievement, type of news organization worked for, and type of career path followed. Friendship patterns that tend to exclude or include nationals of the country of assignment may also be significant at times.

What is striking about these factors is that so few of them, affecting journalists at different points in time, can have such a profound impact on major orientations reflecting the adult professional and strategic beliefs of correspondents. If we know something about the way each of the factors mentioned has affected a journalist, we also know a great deal about what that journalist believes and is likely to think about his reporting role in crisis conditions.

The Professional Orientations of Foreign-Affairs Reporters — Specifically the Examining, Adversarial, and Pluralist Dimensions Outlined in This Survey — Represent an Enduring Set of Internalized Perspectives Resistant to Change

To suggest that foreign affairs reporters carry a set of coherent perspectives to their work as crisis reporters is, in the terms of this study, to ask that special attention be paid to a learning or socialization approach to orientations acquired over the course of a life cycle. Placing so much importance on the socialization process represents a departure from several modern approaches to the study of the attitudes and behavior of reporters. One approach that has received a great amount of attention in recent years is the perspective suggesting that what newspapers print and what reporters think about as guidelines or codes is determined in large part by the organizational processes surrounding them. (J. Epstein, 1973; Sigal, 1973; Argyris, 1974; and Tuchman, 1978.) This study of foreign affairs reporters lends partial credence to the organizational approach because it draws attention to the type of news organization employing a reporter (whether broad market or select market) and to the importance of choosing a particular career path (either solo professional or managerial).

A socialization perspective, however, suggests that in ambiguous situations such as crises, journalists are more apt to rely on what they have learned over the course of their life cycles as individuals than they are to reflect automatically the myriad organizational imperatives surrounding them. Although reporters may employ the notion of "objectivity" as a "strategic ritual" to mitigate deadline pressures or to avoid libel suits and the reprimands of superiors, as some scholars believe (Tuchman, 1972; Phillips, 1977: 65), and although organizational processes may account for patterns displayed by both domestic and foreign affairs reporters a vast proportion of the time, under crisis conditions individuals are faced with significant, immediate, personal choices. A learning or socialization approach expects that in such circumstances, journalists will rely on deeply held professional and strategic orientations to guide their thinking about reporting.

It is possible, as Barbara Phillips urges, that the craft of journalism in itself carries with it concommitant perspectives on the nature of the political world and on the way evidence is used. Phillips suggests that, rather than searching for abstract truth, journalists look for facts which are imminent in the world — readily available and easily located. This kind of perspective may distinguish journalists from social-science researchers, who value highly the search for abstract truth and theoretical knowledge. (Phillips, 1977.) Under crisis conditions, nevertheless, the discrete bits of information journalists find most relevant may be framed or viewed through a grid constructed from orientations affected by prior experience, the prior learning of journalists who rely on principles and maxims from preoccupational and early occupational experience.

Distinct Types of News Organizations May Encourage or Reinforce Some Professional Reporting Perspectives as More Appropriate Than Others

This study reveals that for some professional perspectives, foreign affairs reporters who have spent a great many years working for wire services hold different orientations than those working outside wire services. A plausible explanation for this phenomenon is that wire services are constructed to sell the maximum amount of news to the broadest possible market, and in so doing develop both a set of news standards and organizational principles consistent with those goals. For example, in order to maintain access to news sources in a variety of countries, it is important for a news service to remain on good terms with whatever government is in power in each country, regardless of that government's popular legitimacy. For another example, news values that emphasize speed, breadth, and accuracy, the central ingredients of a chronicler perspective, are useful in generating a vast amount of material relatively free of overt interpretation or analysis.

Under crisis conditions, emphasis on speed, breadth, and accuracy may not help readers place events in historical, social, or political perspective as much as an emphasis on examination and interpretation does. In such circumstances, readers who wish to avail themselves of material rich in analysis may wish to supplement their awareness of wire-service material with reports from other news organizations. Distinct news organizations may be associated with distinct professional perspectives on the part of the reporters those organizations employ. Readers who value a variety of perspectives may wish to seek information emanating from different types of news organizations. This suggestion is similar to what Herbert Gans recommends in *Deciding What's News* when he urges a "multiperspectival" approach to news evaluation (1979), and similar also to what Davison, Shanor, and Yu recommend in their booklet, *News From Abroad,* written for the Foreign Policy Association. They urge that attentive and active foreign policy publics adopt:

> . . . a critical approach to international news: keeping in mind that the American definition of news is not necessarily the same as in other countries . . . (and that information seekers be) well advised to consult several media and not to rely on any single one . . . (and further) that advantage should be taken of supplementary sources other than the news media. (Davison, Shanor, and Yu, 1980: 60.)

The Concept of Individual "Character" or the Individual Hero May Continue to Explain Why Some Journalists Are More Professional than Others

The data collected in this study reveal that "loners" tend to be more adversarial than joiners, in the field, in Latin America, and in Washington, D.C. This analysis also reveals that "solo craftsmen" are more likely to be examiners than are those who have been successful in moving upward within management positions. Managerial reporters with good salaries tend not to be examiners, while solo professional reporters with good salaries do tend to be examiners. It may be refreshing for reporters who revere the special qualities of their occupation to find corroboration for what must be a widely accepted or at least nostalgic professional assumption: A dedicated reporter, working alone, can still make a significant contribution to reporting on foreign affairs.

Conclusion

A focus on the way journalists are socialized to become foreign affairs reporters is an essential tool in making predictions about the way news material is processed under crisis conditions. A learning perspective on the news, like a cultural perspective, draws attention to patterns of newsmaking that appear to endure over a long period of time. Unlike "cultural conventions" or "codes," however, the deeply held professional orientations that individual journalists acquire are less likely to become apparent under the routine circumstances of daily reporting than in the exigencies of crisis coverage. When events are ambiguous, when prior guidelines offer little help, and when institutions and values are changing rapidly, journalists are compelled to rely on their individual professional orientations for assistance in fashioning coherent news perspectives. The responsibilities shouldered by individuals carry dramatic implications for the future of foreign affairs reporting.

Foreign Correspondents Face Special Challenges in the Immediate Future

New dilemmas and difficulties are thrust upon foreign affairs journalists with astonishing rapidity. Abroad, several foreign governments and journalists, most visibly through seminars and conferences organized by UNESCO, have criticized western news institutions, especially wire services, for perpetuating outworn stereotypes and for penetrating regional and local news markets so thoroughly with news processed in the industrialized world. (Smith, 1980.) At home, debates proliferate about appropriate news-gathering toward such controversies as the Soviet invasion of Afghanistan and Iran during the Shah, after the Shah, and during the detention of U.S. hostages there.

New crises will doubtless arise to challenge the most skillful reporters. In the first months of President Reagan's administration, foreign affairs journalists have been compelled to exercise a considerable amount of journalistic autonomy in weighing conflicting claims regarding the political and social context of struggle in El Salvador, together with widely differing accounts about the extent of non-U.S. foreign influence there. The way journalists form coherent views about these critical events will be shaped by their attitudes toward journalism as an occupation, toward officials, and toward the intensity of East-West conflict.

As Individuals with Distinct Learning Experiences, Correspondents Are Likely to Respond to New Challenges in Quite Distinct Ways

Whatever the claims about "herd instincts" and "pack journalism," in which reporters are often accused of filing similar stories from the field, journalists who undergo different learning experiences are likely to view crises differently as well. A learning approach predicts that the professional perspectives employed in crisis situations are likely to be those that are learned gradually, reinforced by distinct events over the course of a reporter's life cycle, in particular by events or choices occurring in the preoccupational and early career periods of a reporter's life.

As a result, those journalists who acquire examining perspectives on the reporting profession, adversarial orientations toward officials, and pluralist perspectives on East-West disagreements are also likely to be "special" journalists, willing to make their own viewpoints and those belived of concern to the general public known to foreign-policy officials. Journalists with divergent family experiences and educational and career path choices are likely to approach crisis reporting in different ways.

The Persistence of Individual Differences among Foreign Affairs Reporters Diminishes Sharply the Likelihood That They Will Agree on a Common Approach to Professionalization in Journalism

For the most part, the reporters this study identified as professionals do not welcome the formation of journalism associations that are as strong or authoritative as those in law or medicine, capable of erecting clear guidelines and standards for journalistic excellence. Although several of this study's "professionals" have earned Master's degrees and may be likely to support advanced education for journalists, they also prefer to remain relatively unencumbered by a strong professional organization and are therefore markedly unlike professionals in some other occupations. In the absence of clear and shared professional guidelines, the best hope for professionalism in reporting on crises abroad lies in the personal beliefs of journalists who have acquired a capacity for autonomous judgment gradually, at different periods in their personal and occupational growth. A significant warning is necessary, however. Critical learning moments in a reporter's past exert a profound impact on the way journalists convert happenings into events and stories, but that conversion process does not take place in a vacuum. Receptive news outlets are of critical importance.

Because the Defense of Professionalism in Foreign Affairs Journalism Rests So Heavily on the Shoulders of Individual Journalist "Solo Craftsmen" (rather than with managers or supervisors), It Is Essential that Multiple News Outlets — whether Newspapers, Weeklies, or Magazines, Remain Functioning as Vibrant Forums for the Presentation of Divergent, Especially Unpopular, Views

In *Common Sense,* authored by Tom Paine, and *The Federalist Papers,* written principally by Alexander Hamilton and James Madison, the founding fathers of the United States expressed their recognition that new sources of information were necessary if colonists, and later citizens, were to become aware of significant choices available to them. Contemporary recommendations that citizens adopt a "multi-perspectival" approach toward news generally (Gans, 1978), and consult several sources on foreign news in particular (Davison, Shanor, and Yu, 1980) reflect a similar concern. With so few news institutions producing so much of what Americans read about foreign affairs, many opportunities for news management and channeling present themselves. In these circumstances, it is essential that the divergent perspectives of individual craftsmen find news outlets.

Unless different perspectives are given their opportunity to confront one another in the marketplace of ideas, citizens cannot make well considered judgments about foreign-affairs events or policies. The different learning pathways journalists follow may give rise to a variety of perspectives on crisis reporting. In a healthy democracy, the "watchdogs" of the Fourth Estate may benefit from citizen vigilance to preserve the vitality of divergent opinions by preserving a multiplicity of news outlets. Given the trend toward fewer major newspapers throughout the United States, the effort to maintain opportunities for diversity represents an endeavor filled with challenge.

The Willingness of Major News Organizations to Defend the Autonomy and Integrity of Their Reporters is a Critical Element in Any Effort to Support Professional Journalism

The power and authority of *The New York Times* and the *Washington Post* are well known. The capacity of each to withstand government pressure is also well established. The New York paper dramatized that capacity by publishing "The Pentagon Papers" and the Washington, D.C. paper did so by supporting Woodward and Bernstein in their investigation of the Watergate controversy. Historical evidence apart, *The Politics of Crisis Reporting* concludes that the nation's most prominent news publishers (including other dailies and weeklies in addition to the *Times* and the *Post*) play a critical role in encouraging the development of professional perspectives. This study documents the profound importance of prominent news institutions in nourishing examining and adversarial perspectives in particular.

With their impact analyzed, it is clear that the nation's elite news institutions bear an awesome responsibility. If they do not assume leadership in promoting professional standards and working environments for journalists, the fate of those standards may be seriously jeopardized. If America's leading news outlets yield to official efforts to restrict the flow of news, we cannot depend on other institutions to hold aloft the banner of journalistic integrity. But if the same elite news institutions recognize the sweep and reach of their responsibility as chief guardians of a special historical tradition, then they will exert Herculean efforts to provide refuge for intrepid reporters whose careers pay tribute to the highest standards of professional journalism.

Notes

1. Total adds to 99% due to rounding.
2. The full list of disciplinary items is found in McLeod and Rush, 1970.

APPENDIX I

Questionnaire on U.S. Journalists Concerned with Latin America

Questionnaire on U.S. Journalists Concerned with Latin America

You are invited to participate in a study of journalists reporting on foreign affairs. Your name has been selected because at some point in your career you have written or edited stories, or written editorials concerning Latin America.

You are asked to complete a questionnaire. Please remember that in this study there are no "correct" or "incorrect" responses, no preconceived visions of "truth" or "falsehood." You are asked simply to register your *personal* opinion about various questions and statements. If an item appears ambiguous, please answer it by thinking about what you do or believe *most of the time.*

To protect your privacy, be assured that responses to this survey will be kept completely confidential. No individual will be associated with any set of responses, It is hoped that most respondents will be available for follow-up personal interviews to enrich information gathered systematically but anonymously through this instrument.

John C. Pollock

APPENDIX I: The Questionnaire
A Survey of Journalists Concerned with Latin America

I.   Background

The following items request information about individual and journalist background. Some of the questions have been placed in the past tense to accommodate respondents who are no longer employed in journalism. Although some of the questions may appear personal, all items are similar to and permit comparison with those used to develop standard profiles of professionals in other occupations. Answers will *never* be associated with any particular individual.

1. How many years of college level study have you had?

   ( )   none   ( )   4 years
   ( )   1 year   ( )   5 years
   ( )   2 years   ( )   6 years
   ( )   3 years   ( )   7 or more years

2. What degrees have you earned? Please list after each degree the date earned, the field of study, and the college or university granting the degree.

   Degree   Date   Field   College or University
   _____   _____   _____   _____
   _____   _____   _____   _____
   _____   _____   _____   _____
   _____   _____   _____   _____

3. How long have you been (were you) a journalist?

   ( )   5 or fewer years   ( )   15 to 17 years
   ( )   6 to 8 years   ( )   18 to 20 years
   ( )   9 to 11 years   ( )   21 to 25 years
   ( )   12 to 14 years   ( )   over 25 years

4. With what type of organization are you now connected? (Check as many as apply) (Please specify which news organization)

	Newspaper	Press assocation or service	Other (Please specify organization and title)
Full-time	_____	_____	_____
Stringer and/or Free-lancer	_____	_____	_____

5. Why did you become a journalist? (Rank three in order of importance: 1 for primary importance, etc.)

   ( )   salary and benefits   ( )   political reasons
   ( )   social duty or obligation   ( )   adventure
   ( )   opportunity to travel   ( )   accident
   ( )   family ties or connections   ( )   other

6. In what areas have you served (Check as many as apply)?

( ) West Europe/Scandinavia   ( ) North Africa
( ) East Europe/Russia   ( ) Sub-Saharan Africa
( ) Central America   ( ) South/Southeast Asia
( ) South America   ( ) East Asia/China
( ) Middle East   ( ) Oceania/Arctic Regions

7. For how many news organizations have you worked, including the present one (if it is a news organization)? Please specify:

Organization	Years
_____	_____
_____	_____

8. How many years of experience in journalism did you have *before* reporting or editing material, or writing editorials concerning Latin America?

_____ years

9. For how many news organizations did you work *before* writing about Latin America?

_____ organizations

10a. For how many years have you written about (did you write about) Latin America?

_____ years

b. From what year to what year?   19___ to 19___

11. Either before, during, or since working as a journalist, what *kinds* of positions have you held in the public or private sectors (e.g., diplomacy, public relations, publishing)?

	Private Sector	Public Sector	Number of Years
Before Journalism	_____	_____	_____
	_____	_____	_____
	_____	_____	_____
	Private Sector	Public Sector	Number of Years
Intermittent or Simultaneous	_____	_____	_____
	_____	_____	_____
	_____	_____	_____
	Private Sector	Public Sector	Number of Years
After Journalism	_____	_____	_____
	_____	_____	_____

12. If you are not now employed in journalism, why did you leave it? Please specify your two most important reasons for leaving.

First reason_____

_____

Second reason_____

_____

13. What is your age? _____ (years) and sex ____male ____female.

14. In what city and state (and if not the U.S.A., country) were you born?

City _____   State _____

15. Your birth order is _____ in a family of _____ children.

16. What is your matrimonial status?

( ) single   ( ) divorced
( ) married   ( ) remarried
( ) widowed   ( ) other

17. Have you ever served in the armed forces of the U.S. or of any other country?

Yes _____   No _____

If yes: How many years active duty _____; How many years in the reserves _____?

18. What is the highest salary you have earned as a journalist (in U.S. dollars)? Check two)

	Base Salary only	Salary plus Living Expenses and Bonus
( ) Under 20,000	( )	( )
( ) 20,000 – 22,499	( )	( )
( ) 22,500 – 24,499	( )	( )
( ) 25,000 – 27,499	( )	( )
( ) 27,500 – 29,999	( )	( )
( ) 30,000 – 32,499	( )	( )
( ) 32,500 – 34,499	( )	( )
( ) 35,000 – 37,499	( )	( )
( ) 37,500 – 39,999	( )	( )
( ) 40,000 – 44,999	( )	( )
( ) 45,000 or more	( )	( )

II.   The Craft of Journalism

This section asks that you think about journalism as a craft, especially a set of codes or conventions guiding the practice of journalism. In each case indicate the response that most nearly approximates your personal opinion.

1. What importance do you assign to the mass media activities listed below? After each statement, indicate whether you consider the activity "essential," "very important," "important," "seldom important," or "not important at all."

	Essential	Very Important	Important	Seldom Important	Not Important At All
A. Discuss national policy while it is still being developed.	____	____	____	____	____
B. Concentrate on news which is of interest to the widest possible public.	____	____	____	____	____
C. Provide analysis and interpretation of complex problems.	____	____	____	____	____
D. Get information to the public as quickly as possible.	____	____	____	____	____
E. Investigate claims and statements made by the government.	____	____	____	____	____
F. Stay away from stories where factual content cannot be verified quickly.	____	____	____	____	____
G. Consider sources not merely as informants but as people whose interests merit protection.	____	____	____	____	____
H. Depict the viewpoints and interests of competing groups, especially those of excluded and underprivileged groups.	____	____	____	____	____

2. Imagine yourself asked to advise a new reporter about the "codes" or "conventions" governing excellence in foreign affairs reporting. What follows is a list of sentences you might use to guide the recruit. In each case mark how important you consider each item of advice.

2. Imagine yourself asked to advise a new reporter about the "codes" or "conventions" governing excellence in foreign affairs reporting. What follows is a list of sentences you might use to guide the recruit. In each case mark how important you consider each item of advice.

	Agree Com-pletely	Agree Some-what	Neither Agree nor Disagree	Disagree Some-what	Disagree Com-pletely
A. Editors and readers are less interested in foreign news *per se* than in what happens to foreigners in our country or to our citizens abroad.	___	___	___	___	___
B. Pay close attention to a "Continuing Big Story": the themes of stories written by other reporters and printed by other media.	___	___	___	___	___
C. Be more concerned with longrun trends than with "events" which can be observed and confirmed.	___	___	___	___	___
D. To tell a successful story, be certain you focus on some item of "Human Interest": something that happened to a well-known person; or something unusual, conflictual, dangerous or disastrous.	___	___	___	___	___
E. It is relatively easy to generate interest in a new topic.	___	___	___	___	___
F. In reports on Latin America, it is appropriate for a news organization to pay special attention to conflict associated with power transfers — elections, coups, revolutions.	___	___	___	___	___

3. Please indicate whether you agree completely, agree, agree somewhat, disagree somewhat, disagree, or disagree completely, with the following statements.

	Agree Com- pletely	Agree	Agree Some- what	Disagree Some- what	Dis- agree	Disagree Com- pletely
A. A journalist should be cer- tified by his professional organization as to qualifica- tions, training, and com- petence.	___	___	___	___	___	___
B. A journalist should not continue to work for a news- paper if he disagrees sub- stantially with its editorial policy.	___	___	___	___	___	___
C. There should be greater subject-matter specializa- tion in journalism (e.g., economics, science, local government).	___	___	___	___	___	___
D. It is all right to take pro- motional or informational trips sponsored by business organizations or government agencies if there are no strings attached.	___	___	___	___	___	___
E. Journalists in a news organization have a legiti- mate claim to help deter- mine that organization's news column content and policies.	___	___	___	___	___	___
F. If a member of a profes- sional, journalism organiza- tion commits an unprofes- sional action (e.g., takes a bribe), he should be disci- plined by the professional organization, regardless of whether or not formal legal action has been taken.	___	___	___	___	___	___

	Agree Completely	Agree Somewhat	Neither Agree nor Disagree	Disagree Somewhat	Disagree Completely
G. For the working journalist, there should be required periodic institutes or refresher courses, *e.g.*, in economics or political science.	____	____	____	____	____	____
H. Professions such as law and medicine have developed organizations to uphold professional standards. Journalists themselves should form an organization to deal with problems that come up, and to supervise the profession.	____	____	____	____	____	____

	Essential	Very Important	Important	Seldom Important	Not Important At All
4. How useful a role do you think crusaders and social reformers play in news media today?	____	____	____	____	____
5. How useful a role do you think counterculture media are playing in the United States today?	____	____	____	____	____

III. News Organizations

The next items request information about the organizational contexts of foreign affairs journalism.

1. Which news organization would you most like to work for as someone writing on foreign affairs?

_____

2. When you reported on the region, which news organization in your opinion did the best job of reporting on Latin America (the news organization you considered the fairest and most reliable)?

_____

3. Compared with the average journalist writing about foreign affairs, how would you view the professional ability of most of your North American colleagues covering the news from Latin America?

____ Substantially better than average; ____ Somewhat better than average; ____ About average; ____ Somewhat below average; ____ A good deal below average.

4. How would you evaluate the performance of the major news organization you worked with at the time in each of the crises you wrote about (from "outstanding" to "very good" to "good" to "fair" to "poor")? (Check as many as apply)

	O	VG	G	F	P	No opin.	Rank
A. The coup in Guatemala in 1954	___	___	___	___	___	___	___
B. The assumption of leadership in Cuba by Fidel Castro in early 1959	___	___	___	___	___	___	___
C. The Bay of Pigs incident in 1961 (before after)	___	___	___	___	___	___	___
D. The 1964 coup in Brazil	___	___	___	___	___	___	___
E. The attempt to restore the government of Juan Bosch in the Dominican Republic in 1965 and sending U.S. Marines there	___	___	___	___	___	___	___
F. The election of Salvador Allende as President of Chile in 1970	___	___	___	___	___	___	___

5. Please return to the crises in question 4 and rank each one according to how much material you wrote about it: "1" for the crisis you wrote most about, "2" for the crisis you wrote somewhat less about, ranking as many as apply.

6. Think about the crisis for which you personally contributed the most amount of written material. Please answer the following appropriate questions.

   A.

   1. If you ranked the news organization between "very good" to "fair": why did you rank the organization as high as you did? Please elaborate (UNLESS RANK IS ALWAYS "POOR"). (Specify events A, B, C, D, and/or E)

   2. Why did you rank the organization as low as you did? Please elaborate (UNLESS RANK IS ALWAYS "OUTSTANDING"). (Specify events A, B, C, D, and/or E.)

   B. IF YOU ALWAYS RANKED "POOR": why did you not rank the organization higher?

   C. IF ALWAYS "OUTSTANDING": why did you not rank the organization lower?

   D. For all respondents to answer: comparing your evaluation of the same news organization(s) with its performance now, how does it differ, if it differs at all?

7. What percentage of your time each week was spent engaged in each of the following activities *during the crisis you wrote most* about?

   ____ Managerial Responsibilities; ____ Editing; ____ Reporting; ____ Editorial Writing; ____ Special Assignments (*e.g.,* a column, reviews, features). 100% total.

8. What percentage of your time each week is spent engaged in the same activities *now*?

   ____ Managerial Responsibilities; ____ Editing; ____ Reporting; ____ Editorial Writing; ____ Special Assignments (*e.g.,* a column, reviews, features).

9. If you have any managerial responsibilities, how many editorial employees altogether report to you either directly or indirectly? (Do not count secretaries.)

____ None; ____ 1–2; ____ 3–5; ____ 6–10; ____ 11–25; ____ More than 25.

10. How much influence do you have on hiring and firing?

____ Ultimate; ____ A large amount; ____ A moderate amount; ____ Little; ____ None.

11. In general, when you wrote about Latin America how did you feel about the emphasis placed by your supervisors on news from that region? (Check only one.)

( ) Received far less play than it deserved
( ) Received somewhat less play than it deserved
( ) Received about the right amount of play
( ) Received somewhat more play than it deserved

12. When you wrote about Latin America, how would you describe the direction you received from your supervisors most of the time? (Check one only.)

( ) Strong direct control over my output and assignments
( ) They had considerable control, but encouraged independent action
( ) Very little control
( ) They exercised virtually no control, leaving the initiative completely with me.

13. Which of these statements best describes the way you felt about your supervisors most of the time) (Check only one.)

( ) I believed I was very much a member of a large, well-organized, cooperative team.
( ) I believed I was part of a team, but much of the time I didn't know what was going on.
( ) Most of the time I believed I was operating as an individual rather than as part of a team.

14. How aware have you been of any particular editorial policies held by your publishers?

Almost Always Aware	Very Aware	Somewhat Aware	Seldom Aware	Almost Never Aware
( )	( )	( )	( )	( )

If you were a correspondent, please answer the following questions. If not, please go to the next page (8-a).

15. How often did you typically file a story or article?

( ) daily; ( ) five times a week; ( ) four times a week; ( ) three times a week; ( ) two times a week; ( ) once a week; ( ) occasionaly; ( ) the amount varies considerably.

16. How did you rate your home office editors in the major news organization you worked with on their ability to evaluate the real news value of your output? (Check only one.)

( ) extremely well qualified; ( ) fairly well qualified; ( ) not particularly well qualified; ( ) poorly qualified.

17. How often did you typically return to the United States? (Check only one.)

( ) More than once every six months; ( ) More than once a year; ( ) Once a year; ( ) Every two years; ( ) Every three years; ( ) Less often.

18. Imagine yourself asked to advise a new reporter about the "conventions" governing excellence in coverage of the State Department. In each case mark how important you consider each item of advice.

	Agree Completely	Agree Somewhat	Neither Agree nor Disagree	Disagree Somewhat	Disagree Completely
A. Reporters should verify information obtained from unauthorized sources in the Department before publication in any form.	___	___	___	___	___
B. Reporters should report the facts avoiding any interpretation whatsoever.	___	___	___	___	___
C. Reporters should bring public views and needs to the attention of Department officers.	___	___	___	___	___
D. Reporters should incorporate statements of Department policy in their material whether they agree or disagree with it.	___	___	___	___	___
E. Reporters should work through Department information officers.	___	___	___	___	___
F. Reporters should write without regard for the editorial views of their news organization.	___	___	___	___	___

IV. The Sources and Working Conditions of Journalism

This section asks you to answer questions about the sources and daily working conditions you have encountered.

1. Which of these statements best describes your personal off-duty social relationships with people in journalism or communications?

____ Most of my close friends and social contacts are journalists.
____ I have many close friendships and social contacts with journalists.
____ There are a few journalists with whom I am on terms of close friendship.
____ While there are journalists whom I see socially, there are none with whom I have a really close friendship.
____ I have virtually no social contacts with journalists except those which are basically professional contacts.

2. What per cent of the people you see each week in off-duty, social relations are:

   A. U.S. government officials ____   B. U.S. business executives ____

3. Do you belong to any journalism associations? Yes ____; No ____.
   IF YES:
   1. How many ____
   2. Please list the names of as many as three associations, indicating whether it is strictly a professional association, a Greek-letter society, or a social organization.
   3. Please list the organizations in the order of their importance to you.
      Most important   a. _____
      Next most important   b. _____
      Least important   c. _____

4. Please specify the three most important *kinds* of sources used when you wrote (write) material on Latin America. Name the kind of organization the source represented and its nationality.

	Organization (e.g., public relations, other newspapers, embassy)	Its Nationality
First in importance	_____	_____
Second	_____	_____
Third	_____	_____

5. Would you describe the relations between reporters and U.S. officials in Washington, D.C., as:

   a. ____ always collegial
   b. ____ usually collegial
   c. ____ somewhat collegial
   d. ____ somewhat adversarial
   e. ____ usually adversarial
   f. ____ always adversarial

6. Would you describe the relations between reporters and U.S. officials stationed in Latin America as:

   a. ____ always collegial
   b. ____ usually collegial
   c. ____ somewhat collegial
   d. ____ somewhat adversarial
   e. ____ usually adversarial
   f. ____ always adversarial

7. What was your *major* source of job satisfaction when writing about Latin America? (Check only one.)

   ____ The political and historical interest of this particular region.
   ____ The challenges and demands made on my skills and talents as a newsman in this assignment.
   ____ Other sources of satisfaction (Specify) _____

8. What kind of employment would you like in the next five years? (Check one.)

   ____ Work for the same News Organization
   ____ Work elsewhere in news media
   ____ Work outside news media

If you were a correspondent, free lancer, or special correspondent reporting from Latin America, please answer the following questions. If you did not hold any of these positions, please turn to Section V.

9. A list of 20 sources is printed below. You are asked to respond to two separate questions by ranking sources in order of their importance to you. Please read the entire list before responding.

   a. When you have just arrived in a country, which of the twenty sources do you rely on *first* (PLEASE RANK THE FIRST THREE IN ORDER OF IMPORTANCE: 1, 2, 3, WHERE 1 IS THE MOST IMPORTANT).

   b. In a breaking story, where time is short and your preferred sources may be unavailable, what three sources out of the total of twenty would you turn to next? (PLEASE RANK THE NEXT THREE ALPHABETICALLY IN ORDER OF IMPORTANCE: A FOR MOST IMPORTANT, B, AND C)

List of Sources	First Arrival Sources (1, 2, 3)	Breaking Story Sources (A, B, C)
A. *Host Country Sources*		
1. Host country government press office bulletins	____	____
2. Host country radio or television	____	____
3. Host country newspapers and magazines	____	____
4. Press briefings by host country	____	____
5. Host country government officials	____	____
6. Host country politicians	____	____
7. Host country businessmen	____	____
8. Host country journalists	____	____
9. "Man in the Street"	____	____
10. Labor leaders	____	____
11 Agricultural workers	____	____
12. Prisoners	____	____
B. *Foreign Sources*		
13. Other foreign correspondents	____	____
14. Foreign diplomats in host country	____	____
15. Foreign journalists in host country	____	____
16. Foreign businessmen	____	____
C. *U.S. Sources*		
17. U.S. Government press releases	____	____
18. Other U.S. journalists	____	____
19. U.S. officials in host country	____	____
20. U.S. businessmen	____	____

10. Which of these statements best describes your personal off-duty social relationships with nationals of the country in which you were stationed? (Check only one.)

    a. ____ Most of my close friends and social contacts were nationals of the country.
    b. ____ I had many close friendships and social contacts with local nationals.
    c. ____ There were a few local nationals with whom I was on terms of close friendship.
    d. ____ While there were local nationals whom I saw socially, there were none with whom I had a really close friendship.
    e. ____ I had virtually no social contacts with local nationals except those which were basically professional contacts.

11. When I was in Latin America, my best friends were usualy (check only one in each group):

    a. (   ) from the United States
       (   ) from Latin American countries
       (   ) from outside the hemisphere

    b. (   ) Spanish or Portuguese speaking
       (   ) English speaking
       (   ) spoke some other language

    c. (   ) also correspondents
       (   ) a reporter from the host country
       (   ) a neighbor
       (   ) member of my club
       (   ) member of a religious group
       (   ) a professional contact
       (   ) an accidental acquaintance
       (   ) other   (Specify _____)

12. What do you estimate was the total period of time you spent traveling outside of your immediate city of assignment in an average year?

    ( ) less than two weeks   ( ) 5 to 6 months
    ( ) two weeks to 29 days   ( ) 7 to 8 months
    ( ) 1 to 2 months   ( ) 9 to 10 months
    ( ) 3 to 4 months   ( ) 11 to 12 months

13. How familiar were you with the major language spoken in the country in which you were stationed? (Check one for reading, one for speaking)

    Reading   Speaking

    ____   ____   Native fluency or close to it
    ____   ____   Easy facility
    ____   ____   Partial familiarity
    ____   ____   Less than partial familiarity

14. With what languages, apart from that (those) of the countries in Latin America you may have reported from, do you have a conversational familiarity?

    1. _____   2. _____   3. _____

V. Opinions About Foreign Policy Goals

In this final section are a number of standard phrases and statements concerning foreign policy goals. You are asked to register your degree of agreement or disagreement with each item. Remember, register the general opinion you hold *most* of the time or in *most* cases.

Please put a check in the appropriate column, regarding to whether you: agree completely, agree somewhat, neither agree nor disagree, disagree somewhat or disagree completely.

	Agree Completely	Agree Somewhat	Neither Agree Nor Disagree	Disagree Somewhat	Disagree Completely
1. The United States should concentrate on keeping itself strong and should not get involved in the affairs of other countries.	___	___	___	___	___
2. The only way peace can be maintained is to keep America so powerful and well armed that no other nation will dare to attack us.	___	___	___	___	___
3. The Organization of American States is largely ineffectual in maintaining hemispheric security.	___	___	___	___	___
4. The United States should give help to foreign countries even if they are not as much against communism as we are.	___	___	___	___	___
5. When a national government is incompetent, the use of economic sanctions against it can be justified.	___	___	___	___	___
6. We should cooperate fully with smaller democracies and should not regard ourselves as their leaders.	___	___	___	___	___
7. Only a show of military strength can prevent the Soviet Union from trying to gain world domination.	___	___	___	___	___

	Agree Com- pletely	Agree Some- what	Neither Agree Nor Disagree	Disagree Somewhat	Disagree Com- pletely
8. Military considerations play too great a role in formulating U.S. foreign policy.	___	___	___	___	___
9. Relinquishing the Panama Canal may reduce substantially the capacity of the United States to maintain peace in the hemisphere.	___	___	___	___	___
10. United States business and economic interests overseas constitute threats to the well-being and sovereignty of many nations.	___	___	___	___	___
11. The United States should keep soldiers overseas where they can help countries that are against communism.	___	___	___	___	___
12. The real enemy today is no longer communism but rather war itself.	___	___	___	___	___
13. U.S. foreign aid contributions should be substantially increased.	___	___	___	___	___
14. In the long run, it would be to our best interest as a nation to spend less money for military purposes and more money for education, housing, and other social improvements.	___	___	___	___	___
15. When a national government is incompetent, the use of force to remove it can be justified.	___	___	___	___	___
16. Development of highly advanced weapons systems increases the chances of war.	___	___	___	___	___

	Agree Com- pletely	Agree Some- what	Neither Agree Nor Disagree	Disagree Somewhat	Disagree Com- pletely
17. The first principle of our foreign policy should be to join forces with any country, even if it is not very democratic, just as long as it is strongly anti- communist.	___	___	___	___	___

National Policy Goals

18. Labor unions should become stronger and have more influence generally.	___	___	___	___	___
19. It is not the government's responsibility to make sure that everyone has a secure job and a good standard of living.	___	___	___	___	___
20. Poverty could be almost entirely done away with if we can make certain basic changes in our social and economic system.	___	___	___	___	___
21. The best political can- didate to vote for is the one whose greatest in- terest is in fighting vice and graft.	___	___	___	___	___
22. All old people should be taken care of by the gov- ernment.	___	___	___	___	___
23. The federal government should attempt to cut its annual spending.	___	___	___	___	___
24. It is the concern of the federal government to in- itiate, direct, and finance relief programs for pover- ty stricken areas.	___	___	___	___	___

APPENDIX II

Code for Factor Analysis in Chapter 7

Dependent Variables	Factors
GUTEXAMB	Examiner
LATADV2	Field Adversary
DCADVER1	Capital Adversary
GUTABRDB	Non-Interventionist
GUTFITEB	Favoring Detente

Independent Variables	Factors
AGE1	Age
BAFIELD1	College Major
HIDEG1	Highest Degree
SIBRAN1	Birth Order
SIBTOT1	Sibling Number
HISAL1	Highest Salary
NOWED1	% Time Editing
ELITE	Employing News Organization (4 categories)
WIRE	Employing News Organization (2 categories)
TEAM1	Team Work Context
METREND	Occupation of Best Friends in Field
TREN1	Forecasts for Improved Reporting

Independent Variables	Factors
NBREMP1	Number of Employees Supervised
LATED1	% Time Field Editing
CHILERO1	Evaluation of Chile Coverage
BUSSATT1	Supervisor Interest in Latin America
PRONBR1	Number of Professional Society Memberships
TRAVEL1	Field Travel Outside Capital Cities
YRWRITE1	Years in Journalism
YJRNLAT1	Years Reporting on Latin America
JRNSOC1	Friendships with Other Journalists
KNWCHIL2	Familiarity with Chile Coverage
YRACMIL1	Years on Active Military Duty
YRLONG1	Longest Number of Years Spent with Any Single Employer
PROSOC	Any Professional Memberships (yes or no)
SOURCE1A	Preferred Field Sources
NEXTEMP1	Preferred Employer After Five Years
BSTFRND1	Best Friends in the Field
LATFRND1	Majority of Friends in the Field
LATFRND1	Majority of Friends in the Field
LANGADD1	Familiarity with Non-Iberian Languages

Examiner Factor Pattern

	FACTOR1	FACTOR2	FACTOR3	FACTOR4	FACTOR5
GUTEXAMB	0.15559	−0.41820	−0.25485	0.32279	0.64217
AGE1	0.49208	0.65847	0.13060	0.29896	0.13982
HIDEG1	0.05744	−0.59146	0.13196	0.41589	−0.16898
SIBTOT1	−0.15106	0.27879	0.05386	−0.68223	0.32074
HISAL1	0.57332	0.30602	0.01672	−0.07568	0.22472
NOWED1	0.14071	0.25094	−0.66604	−0.31115	−0.39409
ELITE	0.82572	−0.35491	−0.04124	−0.16124	−0.24446
WIRE	−0.86909	0.30322	0.00973	0.04897	0.15219
TEAM1	−0.38079	0.41287	−0.22336	0.46363	−0.33583
YRWRITE1	0.40283	0.77843	0.16601	0.26298	0.01874
BSTFRND1	−0.05951	−0.02825	0.82914	−0.15452	−0.24785

Total Variance Explained:
GUTEXAMB
0.78

Field Adversary Factor Pattern

	FACTOR1	FACTOR2	FACTOR3	FACTOR4	FACTOR5
LATADV2	-0.26685	0.46809	-0.32255	0.23443	-0.46549
HIDEG1	-0.42411	-0.04830	-0.24235	0.48322	-0.06698
BAFIELD1	0.41674	-0.32654	0.49016	-0.19997	-0.10002
AGE1	0.00443	0.60416	0.22474	-0.50366	0.05134
ELITE	-0.87904	-0.00256	0.13233	-0.24742	-0.12998
WIRE	0.86843	-0.05845	-0.24048	0.25153	0.00444
NBREMP1	0.31743	0.12934	-0.46406	-0.19223	-0.21848
LATED1	0.17317	0.24797	-0.46690	-0.06342	0.55636
CHILE701	0.50380	0.55282	0.09549	0.19522	-0.28702
BOSSATT1	0.11549	-0.41702	-0.31815	-0.47035	0.21298
PRONBR1	0.34816	0.15780	0.57663	-0.01848	-0.11536
TRAVEL1	-0.42175	0.27706	0.03157	0.01310	0.10346
YJRNLAT1	0.15342	0.75132	0.03118	-0.04509	0.23486
JRNSOC1	-0.03861	-0.15018	0.34750	0.60951	0.40577
KNWCHIL2	-0.19754	0.44125	0.15683	0.06319	0.36866

Total Variance Explained:
LATADV2
0.67

Capital Adversary Factor Pattern

	FACTOR1	FACTOR2	FACTOR3	FACTOR4	FACTOR5
DCADVER1	− 0.03041	0.53482	0.32186	0.26279	0.20473
SIBRANK1	− 0.10967	0.24969	0.50765	− 0.53492	0.12698
SIBTOT1	0.00192	− 0.15490	0.07324	0.82975	− 0.18155
AGE1	0.90606	0.10249	0.08864	0.03022	− 0.03459
AUIUN1	− 0.19467	0.11843	0.58312	0.03002	− 0.20108
LAIBOSS1	0.18659	− 0.25488	− 0.48077	0.08042	0.55707
NBREMP1	0.00227	− 0.58654	0.29187	− 0.12216	0.56761
ELITE	0.01733	0.79475	0.02898	− 0.07059	0.26105
TREN1	− 0.01808	− 0.54117	0.64701	0.15040	0.02405
MEETFRND	− 0.15363	0.34408	0.19928	0.50745	0.41909
YRWRITE1	0.88943	0.02727	0.10929	0.01211	0.03267
YJRNLAT1	0.59418	− 0.26329	0.22958	− 0.07505	0.00998

Total Variance Explained:
DCADVER1
0.50

Non-Intervention Factor Pattern

	FACTOR1	FACTOR2	FACTOR3	FACTOR4	FACTOR5
GUTABRDB	−0.29901	0.63522	0.09582	−0.20133	−0.32038
YRDEG1	−0.82193	−0.17908	−0.04268	0.01469	0.06922
AGE1	0.83480	0.25529	0.18617	−0.08152	−0.16402
BAFIELD1	−0.18362	0.62171	−0.36044	−0.00265	0.10139
HIDEG1	−0.33278	−0.40432	0.53260	0.26625	0.02919
YRACMIL1	−0.09948	0.46596	0.43435	0.28379	−0.33947
HISAL1	0.46178	−0.02120	0.16338	−0.44019	0.41969
YRLONG1	0.80994	0.13544	−0.08675	0.00402	0.12921
LATED1	0.21200	−0.47019	−0.09620	−0.21904	−0.37210
TEAM1	0.26717	−0.33294	−0.31377	0.39169	−0.29181
YJRNLAT1	0.59348	−0.12553	0.22056	0.36436	0.01263
PROSOC	−0.02490	0.06687	−0.52009	0.35022	0.44151
BSTFRND1	0.00131	0.22657	0.41301	0.48273	0.41882
SOURCE1A	−0.15480	−0.13039	0.34192	−0.45164	0.29768

Total Variance Explained:
GUTABRDB
0.64

Detente Factor Pattern

	FACTOR1	FACTOR2	FACTOR3	FACTOR4	FACTOR5
GUTFITEB	−0.48627	−0.09088	0.11446	0.18544	0.55281
AGE1	0.31511	0.69145	0.13482	−0.21718	0.12819
HIDEG1	−0.43250	−0.01010	−0.42802	0.44588	−0.17970
BAFIELD1	0.12106	−0.40459	0.19268	−0.44027	0.14309
SIBRANK1	−0.30625	0.15745	−0.34274	0.27193	0.22387
SIBTOT1	0.21455	−0.13714	0.36066	−0.28473	−0.40968
MARSTAB	0.36030	0.08429	−0.22857	−0.09085	0.17910
HISAL1	−0.08247	0.56791	0.52348	0.18654	−0.01076
NBREMP1	0.28265	−0.03886	0.34044	0.58943	0.09598
ELITE	−0.67765	0.53624	−0.06205	−0.17188	−0.10288
WIRE	0.65446	−0.60181	0.09200	0.23144	−0.01723
YRLONG1	0.47680	0.64197	0.21476	−0.11828	0.06842
TEAM1	0.52331	−0.01284	−0.34212	0.26806	0.30320
NBREIEE1	0.47649	−0.12161	−0.08149	−0.09768	0.31299
YJRNLAT1	0.47511	0.47251	−0.05229	0.26250	−0.16339
NEXTEMP1	−0.03733	0.20348	0.53471	0.31094	0.26217
SOURCE1A	−0.22105	−0.17085	0.19418	0.23403	0.02194
BOSSATT1	−0.15896	−0.22882	0.55813	0.02339	0.09690
LATFRND1	0.31679	0.14772	−0.18238	0.36060	−0.51581
LANGADD1	−0.22535	−0.29117	0.44767	0.20653	−0.30841

Total Variance Explained:
GUTFITEB
0.60

Bibliography

Adler, Norman and Harrington, Charles 1970. *The Learning of Political Behavior.* Glenview, Illinois: Scott, Foresman & Co., p. 66.

"An Exchange on Chile: Robert Schakne and Roger Morris." 1975. *Columbia Journalism Review* (January/February) 56–58.

Aggarwala, N.K. 1979. "What is Development News," *Journal of Communication* 29:2 (Spring) pp. 180–181.

Argyris, Chris 1974. *Behind the Front Page: Organizational Self-Renewal in a Metropolitan Newspaper.* San Francisco: Jossey-Bass Publishers.

Aronson, James 1970. *The Press and the Cold War.* New York: Bobbs-Merrill, pp. 200–202. Chapters 13–18.

_____ . 1972. *Deadline for the Media.* New York: Bobbs-Merrill.

Barnes, J.A. 1968. "Networks and Political Process," in Marc J. Swartz, ed., *Politics: Social and Cultural Perspectives.* London: U. of London Press, Ltd.

Barnes, Peter 1964. "The Wire Services in Latin America," *Neiman Reports* (March) pp.

Batscha, Robert M. 1975. *Foreign Affairs News and the Broadcast Journalist.* New York: Praeger.

Becker, Lee B., Sobowale, Idowu A. and Cobbey, Robin E. 1981. "Reporters and Their Professional and Organizational Commitments," in G. Cleveland

Wilhoit, and Harold deBock, eds. *Mass Communication Review Yearbook.* Vol. 2. Beverly Hills: Sage.

Beltran, Luis Ramiro 1975. "Research Ideologies in Conflict," *Journal of Communication* 2, pp. 187–93.

_____.1976. "Alien Premises, Objects, and Methods in Latin American Communication Research," *Communication Research,* 3:2 (April), pp. 197–234.

Bernstein, Victor and Gordon, Jesse 1967. "The Press and the Bay of Pigs," *Columbia University Forum* (Fall).

Birns, Laurence 1973a. "Requiem for Chile: La Moneda is Burning." In *The Village Voice* (September 20).

_____. 1973b. "The Death of Chile." *The New York Review of Books* (November).

_____. 1973c. "Chile: A Bloody Fall." *Worldview* (November).

_____. 1973d. "Chile in the 'Wall Street Journal'." *The Nation* (December 3).

Blake, Judith 1981. "The Only Child in America," *Population and Development Review,* Volume 7: Number 1 (March), pp. 43–54.

Block, M. 1962. "The Night Castro 'Unmasked'." *Columbia Journalism Review* (Summer): 5–10.

Blumer, Jay and Gurevitch, Michael 1975. "Towards a Comparative Framework for Political Communications Research," in Steven Chaffee, ed., *Political Communication: Issues and Strategies for Research.* Beverly Hills: Sage, p. 193.

Bogart, Leo 1968. "The Overseas Newsman: A 1967 Profile Study." *Journalism Quarterly* 45 (Summer 1968) 293–306.

Bossard, James, and Bowl, Eleanor 1956. *The Large Family System.* Philadelphia: University of Pennsylvania Press.

Braestrup, Peter 1977. *Big Story.* Boulder: Westview Press.

Breed, Warren 1955. "Newspaper 'Opinion Leaders' and Processes of Standardization." *Journalism Quarterly,* p. 283.

Browne, Malcolm W. 1964. "Vietnam Reporting: Three Years of Crisis," *Columbia Journalism Review,* Fall, pp. 4–9.

Campbell, Angus, *et al.* 1960. *The American Voter.* New York: John Wiley & Sons.

Cass, James and Birnbaum, Max 1979. *Comparative Guide to American Colleges.* New York: Harper and Row.

Central Intelligence Agency Press Release 1977. "New C.I.A. Regulations on Relationships with U.S. News Media," (December 2).

Chain, Pat 1973. "Press Coverage of the Chilean Coup: The Information Gap." In *Community Action on Latin America (CALA) Newsletter* (October).

Chittick, William O. 1970. *State Department, Press, and Pressure Groups: A Role Analysis.* New York: Wiley—Interscience.

Clausen, John 1968. "Perspectives on Childhood Socialization," in John Clausen (ed.) *Socialization and Society.* Boston: Little, Brown, and Company.

Cockburn, Alexander 1977. "Don't Forget Your Trenchcoat" in Richard Pollack, ed., *Stop the Presses I Want to Get Off.* New York: Ballantine.

Cohen, Bernard 1963. *The Press and Foreign Policy.* Princeton: Princeton University Press.

Commission on the Freedom of the Press 1947. *A Free and Responsible Press: A General Report on Mass Communication: Newspapers, Radio, Motion Pictures, Magazines, and Books.* Chicago: University of Chicago Press (The "Hutchins Commission Report).

Cooper, Kent 1942. *Barriers Down.* New York: Farrar & Reinhart, Inc.

Cutler, Neal E. 1975. "Toward a Generational Conception of Political Socialization," in David C. Schwartz and Sandra Kenyon Schwartz, eds. *New Directions in Political Socialization.* New York: The Free Press, pp. 254–288.

Dahlgren, Peter 1981. "TV News and the Suppression of Reflexivity," in Eihu Katz, ed. *Mass Media and Social Change.* Beverly Hills: Sage

Davies, James C. 1965. "The Family's Role in Political Socialization," *Annals of the American Academy of Political and Social Sciences.* vol. 361 pp. 10–19.

Davison, W. Phillips 1974. "News Media and International Negotiation," *Public Opinion Quarterly,* 38, pp. 174–91.

_____ . 1975. "Diplomatic Reporting: Rules of the Game," *Journal of Communication* (Autumn) pp. 138–146.

_____ , Shanor and Yu, Frederick, T.C. 1980. *News from Abroad.* New York: Foreign Policy Association.

DeFleur, Melvin L. 1970. *Theories of Mass Communication.* New York: David McKay Co., Inc.

De Sola Pool, Ithiel 1973. "Newsmen and Statesmen: Adversaries or Cronies?" in William L. Rivers and Michael J. Nylan, eds., *Aspen Notebook on Government and the Media.* New York: Praeger.

Dittes, J. and P. Capra 1962. "Affiliation: Comparability or Compatibility," *American Psychologist,* 17, pp. 329–35.

Dunn, D.D. 1969. *Public Officials and the Press.* Reading, Massachusetts: Addison-Wesley.

Elliott, Phillips and Golding, Peter 1973. "The News Media and Foreign Affairs," in R. Boardman and A.J.R. Broom, eds., *The Management of Britain's External Affairs.* London: Macmillan.

Epstein, Edward J. 1973. *News from Nowhere.* New York: Vintage.

Erikson, Erik 1957. *Young Man Luther.* New York: W.W. Norton.

_____ 1968. *Gandhi's Truth.* New York: W.W. Norton.

Falkowski, Lawrence S. 1978. *Presidents, Secretaries of State, and Crises in U.S. Foreign Relations: A Model and Predictive Analysis.* Boulder: Westview.

_____ , ed. 1979. *Psychological Models in International Politics.* Boulder: Westview Press.

Francis, M.J. 1967. "The U.S. Press and Castro: A Study in Declining Relations." In *Journalism Quarterly* (Summer).

Ferry, W.H. 1975. "Masscomm as Guru" in John C. Merrill and Ralph D. Barnery, eds., *Ethics and the Press — Readings in Mass Media Morality.* New York: Hastings House.

Galbraith, John K. 1978. "Global Strategic Thought" in *New York Review of Books,* 201, p. 72.

Galtung, Johan and Ruge, Mari Homboe 1965. "The Structure of Foreign News," in *The Journal of Peace Research* 2:7 pp. 64–91.

Gans, Herbert 1978. *Deciding What's News.* New York: Vintage.

Gardner, Mary A. 1960. *The Inter-American Press Association.* Austin: Institute for Latin American Studies, U. of Texas Press.

Gerbner, George and Marvanyi, George 1977. "The Many Worlds of the World's Press," *Journal of Communication* 27:1 (Winter) pp. 52–66.

Geyer, Georgie Ann 1969. "Latin America: The Making of an 'Uncontinent' " in *Columbia Journalism Review* (Winter), pp. 49–53.

Gilmore, G., and Root, R. 1971. *Modern Newspaper Editing.* Berkeley, California: Glendessary Press.

Gitlin, Todd 1980. *The Whole World is Watching.* Berkeley, California: University of California Press.

Gramling, O. 1940. *A.P.: The Story of the News.* New York: Farrar and Rinehart, Inc.

Greenstein, Fred 1969. *Personality and Politics.* Chicago: Markham Publishing Co.

Halberstam, David 1965. *The Making of a Quagmire.* London: Bodley Head.

——— . 1969. *The Best and the Brightest.* New York: Random House.

Hamilton, J.M. 1977. "Ho-Hum — Latin America." *Columbia Journalism Review* 16 (May/June), pp. 9–10.

Hart, J.A. 1966. "Foreign News in U.S. and English daily newspapers: a comparison," *Journalism Quarterly,* 43, 443–48.

Hermann, Charles, ed. 1972. *International Crises.* New York: The Free Press.

Hess, Robert D. and Torney, Judith V. 1967. *The Development of Political Attitudes in Children.* Chicago: Aldine Publishing Co.

Hess, Stephen 1981. *The Washington Reporters.* Washington, D.C.: Brookings Institute.

Hester, Al 1971. "An Analysis of News Flow from Developed and Developing Nations." *Gazette.* 17:1, pp. 29–43.

——— . 1974. "The News from Latin America via a World News Agency." *Gazette.* 20:2, pp. 82–98.

——— . 1976. "Foreign News on U.S. Television: Seeing Through a Glass Darkly — or Not at All," A paper presented at the Tenth Annual Meeting of the International Association for Mass Communication Research, Leicester, England (September).

Hicks, R., and Gordon, A. 1974. "Foreign news content in Israeli and U.S. newspapers," *Journalism Quarterly.* 51:639–44.

Hirsch, Paul M. 1977. "Occupational, Organizational, and Institutional Models in Mass Media Research: Toward an Integrated Framework." in Paul M. Hirsch, *et al.*, eds., *Strategies for Communication Research.* Beverly Hills: Sage Publications, pp. 13–42.

Hohenberg, John 1964. *Foreign Correspondence.* New York: Columbia University Press.

Horton, Philip, ed. 1978. *The Third World and Press Freedom.* New York: Praeger.

Hoyer, Svennik, Hadenius, Stig and Weibull, Lennart 1975. *The Politics and Economics of the Press: A Developmental Perspective.* (Contemporary Political Sociology Series 06–009) Beverly Hills: Sage Publications.

Janowitz, Morris 1975. "Professional Models in Journalism: The Gatekeeper and the Advocate." *Journalism Quarterly* 52:4 (Winter) pp. 618–626, 622.

Johnstone, John W.C., Slawski, Edward J. and Bowman, William W. 1976. *The News People: A Sociological Portrait of American Journalists and Their Work.* Urbana: U. of Illinois Press.

Kennedy, Paul B. 1957. "Problems of Reporting on Latin America," *Neiman Reports* July), pp. 5–6.

Klicsch, Ralph 1975. "A Vanishing Species: The American Newsman Abroad," *Overseas Press Club Membership Directory.* New York: Overseas Press Club.

Kraft, Joseph 1958. "Washington's Most Powerful Reporter," *Esquire.* (November).

Knightley, Peter 1975. *The First Casualty.* New York: Harcourt Brace Janovich, Inc.

Knudson, Jerry 1974a. "Allende Falls; The Press Reacts." *Masthead.* (January).

———. 1974b. "Neruda and Picasso: A Tale of Two Obituaries," *Columbia Journalism Review,* 12, 27–30.

———. 1974c. "Whatever Became of the Pursuit of Happiness: The U.S. Press and Social Revolution in Latin America," *Gazette* 20, pp. 201–24.

———. 1978. *Herbert L. Matthews and the Cuban Story, Journalism Monographs* 54 (February).

Kruglak, Theodore Edward 1974. *The Foreign Correspondents: U.S. Correspondents Based in Europe in the Early 1950's.* Geneva: Librarie E. Droz, 1955. (Reprinted in 1974 by Greenwood Press; Westport, Connecticut).

Langton, Kenneth 1969. *Political Socialization.* New York: Oxford University Press.

Leggett, J.C., Vidi De James, Deborah, Somma, Joseph and Menendez, Tom 1978. *Allende: His Exit and Our Times.* New Brunswick, New Jersey: New Brunswick Cooperative Press.

Lent, John 1977. "Foreign News in American Media," *Journal of Communication,* 27, pp. 46–51.

Levinson, Daniel 1957. "Authoritarian Personality and Foreign Policy," in *Journal of Conflict Resolution,* 1957, 1 pp. 37–47.

Lewis, Howard 1960. "The Cuban Revolt Story," *Journalism Quarterly,* 37, pp. 573–8.

Loory, Stuart 1974. "The CIA's Use of the Press: A 'Mighty Wurlitzer'," *Columbia Journalism Review* 13:3 (September/October) pp. 9–18.

Lutzker, David R. 1960. "Internationalism as a Predictor of Cooperative Behaviorism," *Journal of Conflict Resolution* 4 (4), pp. 426–430.

Lyford, Joseph P. 1962. "The 'Times' and Latin America." In *Center for the Study of Democratic Institutions.* Reprinted in the *Columbia Journalism Review.*

MacEoin, Gary 1974. *No Peaceful Way: Chile's Struggle for Dignity.* New York: Sheed and Ward.

Markel, Lester, ed. 1949. *Public Opinion and Foreign Policy.* New York: Harper and Bros.

Markham, James W.A. 1959. *A Comparative Analysis of Foreign News in Newspapers of the United States and South America.* University Park, Pennsylvania: Penn State Press.

Matthews, Herbert L. 1971. "Cuba and 'The Times,' " in Herbert Matthews, *A World in Revolution.* New York: Scribner's, 337–365.

Mattleart, A. 1974. *Cultura Como Empresa Multinacional,* Mexico, D.F.: Ediciones Era.

May, Ernest 1962. "The Nature of Foreign Policy: The Calculated Versus the Axiomatic," *Daedalus* 91 (Fall) pp. 653–667.

McLeod, Jack M. and Hawley, Searle E. Jr. 1964 "Professionalization Among Newsmen," *Journalism Quarterly* 41:4 (Fall) pp. 529–539.

McLeod, Jack and Rush, Ramona, R. 1969a, 1969b. "Professionalization of Latin American and U.S. Journalists" (in two parts) *Journalism Quarterly* 46:3 (Fall) pp. 583–590; and 46:4 (Winter) pp. 784–789.

McQuail, Dennis 1972. *Sociology of Mass Communications.* Baltimore: Penguin Books.

Merrill, John C. 1968. *The Elite Press and Great Newspapers of the World.* New York: Pitman.

_____ ., John C. 1977. *The Existential Journalist.* New York: Hastings House.

Merrill, John C., Bryan, C.R. and Alisky, M. 1970. *The Foreign Press: A Survey of the World's Journalism.* Baton Rouge: Louisiana State University Press.

Molotch, Harvey and Lester, Marilyn 1974. "News as Purposive Behavior: On the Strategic Use of Routine Events, Accidents, and Scandals," *American Sociological Review,* 39: 101–112.

Morris, Roger, with Mueller, Shelly and Jelin, William 1974. "Through the looking glass in Chile: coverage of Allende's regime," *Columbia Journalism Review.* 13:4 (November/December), pp. 15–24.

Mowlana, Hamid 1975. "Who Covers America." *Journal of Communication* 25 (Summer) pp. 86–91.

Mueller, Claus 1973. *The Politics of Communication.* New York: Oxford University Press.

Nayman, Oguz, B. 1973. "Professional Orientations of Journalists: An Introduction to Communication Analysis Studies," *Gazette* 19:4 pp. 195–212.

Nordenstreng, Kaarle 1979. "Behind the Semantics — A Strategic Design," *Journal of Communication* 29:2 (Spring) p. 195–198.

Omara, R. 1977. "Latin America: The Hole in the News," *Nation* 221 (July 5: 16–18.

Paige, Glenn 1968. "Comparative Case Analysis of Crisis Decisions: Korea and Cuba," in Charles Hermann, ed., *International Crises: Insights from Behavioral Research.* New York: Free Press, pp.

Paletz, David, and Entman, Robert 1981. *Media, Politics, and Power in America.* New York: The Free Press.

Patterson, Eugene, and Kirkpatrick, Clayton 1978. "Statements" before the Subcommittee on Oversight, U.S. House of Representatives Permanent Select Committee on Intelligence, Washington, D.C. (January 5).

Pearson, Ted 1973. "Coverage of Allende: Preconceived, Wishful View." *Chicago Journalism Review.* (November) pp. 3–5.

Peterson, Sophia 1979. Newspaper Gatekeepers and Criteria of News Worthiness for Foreign News. *Journalism Quarterly.*

_____ . 1981. "International News Selection by the Elite Press: A Case Study" *Public Opinion Quarterly* vol.: 45 (Summer) pp. 143–163.

Phillips, Barbara E. 1977. "Approaches to Objectivity: Journalistic vs. Social Science Perspectives," in Paul M. Hirsch, Peter V. Miller, and F. Gerald Kline, eds., *Strategies for Communication Research.* Beverly Hills: Sage Publications, pp. 63–78.

Pollack, Richard 1977. *Stop the Presses, I Want to Get Off.* New York: Ballantine.

Pollock, John 1973a. "Reporting on Chile: What the Press Leaves Out" *The Nation,* January 29, 1973, pp. 134–138.

_____ . 1973b. "The New Cold War in Latin America: The U.S. Press and Chile," in Dale Johnson, ed., *The Chilean Road to Socialism.* New York: Doubleday.

Pollock, John and Dickinson, Torry 1974. "Apologists for Terror: The Chilean Junta and the U.S. Press." *Worldview* (March) pp. 27–32. Reprinted in Gary MacEoin, ed., *Chile Under Military Rule.* New York: International Documentation Center (IDOC).

Pollock, John C., White, Dan, and Gold, Frank 1975a. "When Soldiers Return: Combat and Political Alienation Among White Vietnam Veterans," in David Schwartz and Sandra Kenyon Schwartz, eds., *New Directions in Political Socialization.* New York: The Free Press, pp. 317–333.

Pollock, John Crothers 1975b. "Early Socialization and Elite Behavior," in David Schwartz and Sandra Schwartz, eds., *New Directions in Political Socialization.* New York: The Free Press.

_____ . 1978. "An Anthropological Approach to Mass Communication Research: The U.S. Press and Political Change in Latin America." *Latin American Research Review* 13, pp. 158–62.

_____ . 1980a. "Reporting on Critical Events Abroad: U.S. Journalism and Chile," *Studies in Third World Societies* No. 10.

Pollock, John Crothers and Guidette, Christopher L. 1980b. "Mass Media Crisis, and Political Change: A Cross-National Approach" in Dan Nimmo, ed. *Communication Yearbook 4,* New Brunswick: Transaction Books, pp. 310–324.

Raymond, Jack 1976. "Introduction," *Overseas Press Club Membership Directory.* New York: Overseas Press Club, p. 6.

Renshon, Stanley Allen 1975. "Birth Order and Political Socialization," in David Schwartz and Sandra Schwartz, eds., *New Directions in Political Socialization.* New York: The Free Press, pp. 69–95.

Reston, James 1966. *The Artillery of the Press: Its Influence on American Foreign Policy.* New York: Harper and Row.

_____ . 1972. "The Press, the President, and Foreign Policy," in Charles S. Steinberg, ed., *Mass Media and Communication.* New York: Hastings House.

Reyes Matta, Fernando 1979. "The Latin American Concept of News," *Journal of Communication* 29:2 (Spring), p. 164–171.

Righter, R. 1978. *Whose News? Politics, the Press, and the Third World.* New York: Times Books.

Rivers, William L. 1965. *The Opinion Makers: The Washington Press Corp.* Boston, Beacon Press.

Robinson, Gertrude V. and Sparkes, Vernon M. 1977. "International News in the Canadian and American Press: A Comparative News Flow Study," *Gazette* 22:4 (Spring) 203–218.

Robinson, John P., Rush, Jerrold G. and Head, Kendra 1968. *Measures of Political Attitudes.* Ann Arbor: Survey Research Center (University of Michigan).

Rogers, Everett M. 1976. "Communication and Development: The Passing of the Dominant Paradigm," *Communication Research* 3, pp. 213–40.

Rosenau, James 1969. *International Politics and Foreign Policy.* New York: The Free Press.

_____ . 1971. *The Scientific Study of Foreign Policy.* New York: The Free Press.

Rosenblum, Mort 1977. "Reporting from the Third World," *Foreign Affairs* 55:815–35.

Rosengren, Karl Erik 1977. "International News: Four Types of Tables," *Journal of Communication* 27:1 (Winter) pp. 67–75.

Roshco, Bernard 1975. *Newsmaking.* Champagne-Urbana: University of Illinois Press.

Rosten, Leo 1974. *The Washington Correspondents.* New York: Harcourt, Brace, 1937; or Arno Press, 1974.

Rubin, Bernard 1978. *Questioning Media Ethics.* New York: Praeger.

Salisbury, Harrison 1980. *Without Fear or Favor: The New York Times and It's Times,* N.Y.: New York Times Books, 1980.

Sande, O. 1971. "The Perception of Foreign News." *Journal of Peace Research* 8:221–37.

Schakne, Robert 1976. "Chile: Why We Missed the Story." *Columbia Journalism Review* 14:6 (March/April) pp. 60–62.

Schiller, H. 1973. *The Mind Managers.* Boston: Beacon Press.

Schiltz, Timothy, Sigelman, Lee and Neal, Robert 1973. "Perspective of Managing Editors on Coverage of Foreign Policy News," *Journalism Quarterly* 50:4 (Winter) pp. 716–721.

Schwartz, David 1973. *Political Alienation.* New York: Aldine.

Schwartz, David and Schwartz, Sandra Kenyon 1975. *New Directions in Political Socialization.* New York: The Free Press.

Sears, R.R., Maccoby, E.E. and Levin, H. 1957. *Patterns of Child Rearing.* Evanston, Illinois: Row, Peterson

Semmel, A.K. 1976. "Some Distribution Characteristics of Foreign News Reporting in Four Elite Newspapers." Paper presented at the annual meetings of the International Studies Association, Toronto, Canada, February 25–29.

Seymour-Ure, Colin 1968. *The Press, Politics and the Public.* London: Methuen.

_____ . 1974. *The Political Impact of Mass Media.* London: Constable.

Shudson, Michael 1978. *Discovering the News: A Social History of American Newspapers*. New York: Basic Books.

Siegel, Roberta S. 1965. "An Exploration into Some Aspects of Political Socialization: School Children's Reactions to the Death of a President," in Martha Wolfstein and Gilbert Kilman, eds., *Children and the Death of a President*. New York: Doubleday, pp. 30–61.

Sigal, Leon V. 1973. *Reporters and Officials*. Lexington: D.C. Heath.

Smith, Anthony 1980. *The Geopolitics of Information*. New York: Oxford University Press.

Smith, R.F. 1969. "On the structure of foreign news: a comparison of the *New York Times* and the Indian White Papers," *Journal of Peace Research* 6:23–36.

_____ . 1971. "U.S. news and Sino-Indian relations: an Extra Media Study," *Journalism Quarterly* 48:447–58.

Snyder, Richard C., Bruce, H.W., and Sapin, Burton 1969. "The Decision-Making Approach to the Study of International Politics," in James Rosenau, ed., *International Politics and Foreign Policy*. New York: The Free Press.

Stillman, D. 1970. "Tonkin: What Should Have Been Asked," *Columbia Journalism Review,* 9, pp. 21–27.

Stotland, E. and Cottrell, N.B. 1962a. "Similarity of Performance as Influenced by Interaction, Self-Esteem, and Birth Order," *Journal of Abnormal and Social Psychology,* 64, 183–91.

Stotland, E. and Dunn, R. 1962b. "Empathy, Self-Esteem, and Birth Order," *Psychological Monographs* 76.

_____ . 1963a. "Identification, Opposition, Authority, Self-Esteem, and Birth Order," *Journal of Abnormal and Social Psychology,* 66, pp. 532–40.

Stotland, E., and Walsh, K. 1963b. "Birth Order and an Experimental Study of Empathy," *Journal of Abnormal and Social Psychology.* 66 pp. 610–614.

Sussman, L. 1977. "The 'March Through the World's Mass Media," *Orbis* 20:857 –79.

Szulc, Tad 1965. *Dominican Diary*. New York: Quadrangle Books.

Talese, Gaye 1966. *The Kingdom and the Power*. New York: New American Library.

Thomson, James C. Jr. 1978. "Journalistic Ethics: Some Probings by a Media Keeper," *Neiman Reports* 31:4/32:1 (Winter/Spring 1978), reprinted in Bernard Rubin, ed., *Questioning Media Ethics*. New York: Praeger.

Trento, Joe and Roman, Dave 1977. "The Spies Who Came in From the Newsroom," *Penthouse.* 8:12 (August) pp. 44–50.

Tuchman, Gaye 1972. "Objectivity as Strategic Ritual: An Examination of Newsmen's Notions on Objectivity," *American Journal of Sociology* 77:4 (January) pp. 660–679.

_____ . 1977. "The Exception Proves the Rule: The Study of Routine News Practice," in Paul M. Hirsch, *et al.*, *Strategies for Communication Research*. Beverly Hills: Sage Publications, pp. 43–62.

_____ . 1978. *Making News: A Study in the Construction of Reality*. New York: MacMillam Publishing.

Tunstall, Jeremy 1972. "News Organization Goals and Specialist Newsgathering Journalists," in Dennis McQuail, ed., *Sociology of Mass Communications.* Baltimore: Penguin Books.

_____ . 1974. *Journalists at Work.* Beverly Hills: Sage.

Waugh, Evelyn 1937. *Scoop* Boston: Little, Brown, & Co.

Weisberger, Bernard 1961. *The American Newspaperman,* Chicago: University of Chicago Press.

Weiss, C.H. 1974. "What America's Leaders Read." *Public Opinion Quarterly* 38: 1–22.

Welch, S. 1972. "The American Press and Indochina, 1950–1956." pp. 207–31 in R.L. Merritt (ed.), *Communication in International Politics.* Urbana: University of Illinois Press.

White, David 1950. "The 'Gate Keeper': A Case Study in the Selection of News," *Journalism Quarterly* 27, pp. 383–90.

Whitlow, S. Scott, and Van Tubergen, Gary N., 1978/79. "Patterns of Ethical Decisions Among Investigative Reporters," *Mass Comm Review* Vol. 6:1 (Winter) pp. 2–9.

Wilensky, Harold 1964. "The Professionalization of Everyone?" *American Journal of Sociology.* 70:2 (September) pp. 137–158.

Wilhelm, John 1963. "The Re-Appearing Foreign Correspondents: A World Survey," *Journalism Quarterly* 40 (Spring) pp. 147–168.

Witcover, J. 1970. "Where Washington Reporting Failed," *Columbia Journalism Review,* 9, pp. 7–12.

Wolfstein, Martha and Kliman, Gilbert, eds. 1965. *Children and the Death of a President: Multidisciplinary Studies.* New York: Doubleday.

Yu, Frederick, T.C. and Luter, John 1964. "The Foreign Correspondent and His Work," *The Columbia Journalism Review* (Spring) 5–12.

Zeitlin, Maurice and Scheer, Robert 1960. "The Paper Curtain," in M. Zeitlin and R. Scheer, *Cuba: Tragedy in Our Hemisphere.* New York: Grove Press, appendix 4.

Zimbardo, P. and Formica R. 1963. "Emotinal Comparison and Self-Esteem as Determinants of Affiliation," *Journal of Personality.* 33 pp. 141–62.

Index

Index

About the Author

JOHN CROTHERS POLLOCK, Director of Research, Research & Forecasts, Inc.

Dr. Pollock (B.A., Swarthmore; M.P.A., Syracuse; Ph.D., Stanford) taught political science, sociology, and mass communications both at Rutgers University and at Queens College, City University of New York. He spent one year at the Johns Hopkins School of Advanced International Studies, completed surveys in India and Latin America, and is currently a Research Associate of the Journalism Resources Institute at Rutgers.

Dr. Pollock served as director of the Latin American Institute at Rutgers and as the first chairman of the Committee on the U.S. Press and Latin America of the Latin American Studies Association. He has received several grants from the Social Science Research Council and has published articles on political socialization, mass media and politics, and mass media and social change in scholarly journals and books, including *The Nation, Society, Journalism Quarterly, Worldview,* and *Communications Yearbook.*

Dr. Pollock is currently Director of Research for Research & Forecasts, Inc., a New York based survey research organization. He has supervised several national studies on *Aging in America, The Figgie Report on Fear of Crime: America Afraid,* and *The Connecticut Mutual Life Report on American Values in the 80's: The Impact of Belief.*